SAFE *to be* SEEN *and* HEARD

BY
MICHAELA JONES

Conscious Dreams
PUBLISHING

Safe to be Seen and Heard

Copyright © 2025: Michaela Jones

All rights reserved. No part of this publication may be produced, distributed, or transmitted in any form or by any means, including photocopying, recording, or other electronic or mechanical methods, without the prior written permission of the publisher, except in the case of brief quotations embodied in critical reviews and certain other non-commercial uses permitted by copyright law.

I have tried to recreate events, locales and conversations from my memories of them. In order to maintain their anonymity in some instances I have changed the names of individuals and places, I may have changed some identifying characteristics and details such as physical properties, occupations and places of residence.

Published by Conscious Dreams Publishing
www.consciousdreamspublishing.com

Edited by Elise Abram
Typeset and E-book formatting by Amit Dey
Cover Designed by Emily's World of Design

ISBN: 978-1-917584-17-3

Contents

Introduction v

CHAPTER 1: Silent Cries, Hidden Wounds 1

CHAPTER 2: Unspoken Pain 7

CHAPTER 3: Crying out Unheard 13

CHAPTER 4: Dealers, Drugs and Depression 21

CHAPTER 5: Silent Battles, Empty Echoes 33

CHAPTER 6: Breaking Away 53

CHAPTER 7: Reclaiming Myself 59

CHAPTER 8: Nasty Dex, Nice Dex 65

CHAPTER 9: New Adventures Down Under 73

CHAPTER 10: Bienvenue á Emotional Abuse 83

CHAPTER 11: The Second Time Around 95

CHAPTER 12: Echoes of Past Errors 103

CHAPTER 13: New Zealand, New Problems 117

CHAPTER 14: The Tower Is Crumbling 123

Chapter 15: The Tower Has Fallen 129
Chapter 16: B Is for Bullshit 133
Chapter 17: Recalibration in the Riviera 153
Chapter 18: Cruising, Caribbean & Chaos 161
Chapter 19: Pathways to Profit 167
Chapter 20: The Termination 173
Chapter 21: Fresh Choices, Fresh Paths 181
Chapter 22: Tears on the Chicago Skyline 189
Chapter 23: And Now, The Healing Can Begin 197
Chapter 24: The Road to Renewal 207
Acknowledgments 217
About the Author 219

Introduction

Hi! I'm Michaela.

'Safe to Be Seen and Heard' is a raw, authentic account of my life experiences from sexual abuse, drugs, depression, financial scarcity, and toxic relationships. It's not just a book for those who have suffered sexual abuse, poor mental health and low self-worth, it's a book for anyone who finds themselves repeating negative patterns in their life because of childhood trauma. If you know someone like this, I hope this book helps you understand them better.

After being sexually abused at five years old and keeping it a secret for most of my life, it caused damage. It flooded into every aspect of my life, and I just couldn't understand why bad things kept happening to me. I didn't understand why I found myself trapped in a cycle of painful relationships, repeated disappointments, and constant abandonment and rejection.

Unaware of what was happening to me, I didn't realise I was creating trauma bonds with men who didn't have my best interest at heart. Trauma bonds imprison us in toxic behavioural patterns that continually create negative experiences in our lives.

My intention is to show you through my story how the body and mind store trauma, influencing us to live small and hide our light from the world. If you are suffering from the pain of your past trauma, I hope this book encourages and inspires you to start healing from negative life experiences, break the patterns that are causing you so much pain, and begin to consciously create a new life path. One that is full of joy, happiness, peace, love and success

Trigger Warning - This book makes direct references to childhood sexual abuse, drugs, depression, violence and abortion. Readers who may be sensitive to these elements, please take note if you choose to continue reading.

CHAPTER 1

Silent Cries, Hidden Wounds

I genuinely believed I was special in that boy's eyes. He was a teenager, and I was a primary school child. I believed he had 'chosen' me because he liked me. I didn't understand sexual abuse back then, and I certainly had no idea I was a victim of it at the time. The abuse happened in my home when he came over to hang out with my brothers. If I had ever seen him outside of my home, I would have been with an adult because I was too young to be wandering anywhere by myself. We also didn't go to the same school because he was in secondary, and I was in primary. My home was the only place he could gain access to me. My home was also the only place in the world where I was supposed to feel safe. After violating both my body and my home environment, I learnt very quickly, at such a young age, that I was not safe anywhere. I adopted a personality of being reactive to things and jumped to wrong conclusions frequently based on my experience of not feeling safe. I always assumed the worst-case scenario and reacted impulsively, aggressively, and defensively to almost anything that came up in my life.

I didn't enjoy it when the pervert touched my body and put my hand on his penis, but I thought this was what I had to do because he was older, and I always had to do what older people told me to do. That's the life of a child: constantly being told what to do, how to think, and how to act, as if I had a personality or voice of my own back then to say 'no'. All I knew was that I didn't like it, and I felt dirty and disgusting.

I froze every time he touched me. I didn't suck his penis when he forced it into my mouth because my five-year-old brain had no idea what to do with it, and yet, somehow, he still seemed satisfied, looking down at me and holding my head there until he allowed me to run off and scrub my mouth with toothpaste. I really didn't understand that boy—like, what was he getting from it? I didn't do anything to attract him to me, and yet, he wouldn't leave me alone.

There was a feeling of dread every time he suggested a game of Hide-and-seek. Looking back now, what older teenage boy wants to play that game, especially with younger children? The game was his cue to abuse me in a hidden place. I tried to hide with one of my brothers, but either I couldn't find them or was told I couldn't hide there. Not that any of this falls to them; they had no idea a perverted predator was looking to get his penis into a five-year-old.

I never hid in the same place twice when we played the game because once he knew where I had hidden, he went back to that place the next time we played. When we moved into our new house, the pervert took advantage of the fact that the place was like a building site with stuff everywhere, providing him with more dark corners to get his dick out and touch me.

I'm not sure how that boy ended up befriending my brothers and coming over to play computer games (as well as hide-and-seek when he could get away with it) because he was a fair bit older than them. I'm not sure if the intention was to get inside the house so he could abuse me or if he genuinely wanted to hang out with younger kids, and when he saw me, he seized an opportunity. Either way, it didn't really matter—he shouldn't have had his filthy hands on a five-year-old.

We had a Sega Mega Drive at the time, and we all liked to play *Sonic the Hedgehog* and *Echo the Dolphin*. It was during these games that the perv would sit back behind whoever was playing the game, wrap my hand around his already erect penis, and begin masturbating. It never went on for very long as it was too risky, which makes me wonder why he even bothered. What pleasure did he actually get from it? It was easy to hide what was happening as he pulled me to sit next to him and placed a coat over his lap so nobody could see. It wouldn't have worked if we were all adults, but as my brothers and I were all primary school children, it was easier to get away with.

I remember scrubbing my hands until they were raw, desperately trying to cleanse myself of the shame and disgust my hands had been contaminated with. He often saw me washing my hands, but he never said anything. He must have known I felt disgusting, but then, he, too, was disgusting, so perhaps he felt nothing.

I don't remember him ever talking to me. I don't remember how it all started. All I remember was feeling terrified of him, yet feeling obligated to do as he wanted. I don't know why, but I thought I would get into trouble if I spoke out against him. I think it was because he was older, and I assumed I had to do as he wanted when he wanted.

I could tell he didn't want anyone to know because of the way he touched me when nobody was looking, like it was something between the two of us, although I was confused as to why he completely ignored me at other times. I somehow knew we had to keep it a secret, even though I didn't like it or feel good about any of it, and I unconsciously went along with whatever he wanted.

It seems crazy to say this now as an adult, but back then, I thought he liked me. I thought he did those things to me because I meant something to him. It confused me every time he left the house and didn't say goodbye or acknowledge me in any way after he had been physical with me, and I didn't understand what all that behaviour meant. It was horrible when I saw him out with his friends, and he completely blanked me as if he didn't know me.

This is where the first behavioural patterns were developed. I 'learnt' that I could give a man what he wanted, but I was not good enough or loveable enough to receive anything back. I was just useless. Maybe if I were better, he would be nicer to me. He seemed to have a lot of friends, so I thought I must be lucky that he had chosen me, but I was still not good enough to make him be nice to me.

So, what did I do?

Nothing.

I know he wanted 'us' to be a secret, so I wasn't going to tell anyone because he'd never be nice to me then. I had to do as I was told, and maybe, one day, he would be nice to me and stop hurting my body and my feelings. Obviously, that never happened. I just wasn't good enough. I only served one purpose, and that was to give him access to my body and be quiet about it.

Around the same time, I experienced consistent daily teasing from my dad and brothers, telling me how ugly I was. I was called ugly multiple times a day. Not only was I being physically abused by someone who was allowed into my home, but my family also didn't think I was good enough. And when I cried (which happened a lot), I was made fun of and teased for being a baby. That was where all of those already developed feelings of being unsafe within myself and my home accelerated.

I needed help and support, but I didn't know how to ask for it back then. I didn't feel safe to ask because I believed they would make fun of me again. I spent a lot of my childhood hidden away in my bedroom. I imagined running away. What would I pack? Where would I go? I wanted to take our dog, Max, with me, so it needed to be somewhere he would like, too. I used to look out of my bedroom window across the field to the trees and hills in the distance and wonder what was beyond them and how I could get there. The overwhelming feelings of being alone, unsupported, and misunderstood were present every single fucking day. Only in my imagination could I get some respite from the shit.

It is said that, from the ages of two to six, children operate in their theta brainwaves, meaning they don't have rational or critical thinking and are, therefore, likely to accept whatever they are being told. Things said to or experienced by the child go straight to the subconscious mind and likely remain buried there forever unless an intervention, such as a healing, takes place. It was during this time that I developed the belief that males were dangerous, and they would only take from me without giving anything back in return. I also believed that complying with a male and giving him what he wanted would make me a good girl, and I was simply carrying out a female's duty.

I could try to psychoanalyse this until the cows come home, but it wouldn't do any good when it really is as simple as knowing how the brain works and recognising that the human body stores trauma. Beliefs buried in your subconscious and trauma stored in your body come out in various ways throughout your life, be it behavioural patterns or illnesses.

CHAPTER 2

Unspoken Pain

I don't remember how, when, or why the pervert stopped coming over to the house—I'm really not sure—but he disappeared, and I didn't see him again. I buried all memories of him deep in my subconscious until my teenage years, when the odd memory sporadically popped up out of nowhere, which I masked over with drugs and booze. I was in my early twenties when the pervert's ex-girlfriend and kids came into my life.

The pervert's ex-girlfriend had begun socialising in my local pub, sometimes bringing her kids with her, and I was confronted by this familial connection back to him. I hated it. The ex was a really lovely girl (younger than the pervert, obviously), but I hated it when she talked to me. She always struck up a conversation with me, and it made me feel so uncomfortable. I think she thought I was rude but talking with her filled me with pain and anxiety. To me, she was him, her kids were him and their presence in my local pub was like his presence in my home all over again. Once again, I could do nothing to stop it from happening. She seemed a decent girl, and her kids seemed well-brought-up, which made it harder to comprehend because the pervert had not been a nice person to me. It didn't make sense that someone like him could have had a relationship with a beautiful, sweet woman and produce such lovely kids.

I was overwhelmed with feelings of unfairness that he had people like that in his life when I believed he didn't deserve it. It seemed as if he had been given a free pass to go ahead and enjoy his life surrounded by great people and live free of remorse and/or regret. Thankfully, I moved away from Somerset to Bristol not long after they started coming over to my local pub, so I didn't need to see them any further, and I could go back to being in severe denial.

Although the pervert had suddenly disappeared and went off to live his life without regret or remorse, I was left with all the emotional scars he had forced upon me. These manifested as my being a bully at school. I didn't realise it at the time, but as an adult reflecting back, I can see I was acting out of an unresolved trauma response. I also see why labelling kids as being 'bad' is not useful at all. If kids exhibit 'bad' behaviour, there is a root cause that needs to be addressed instead of dismissed.

I went to a small village school. It was there I took my unspoken trauma out on my peers. Sometimes, I hit them. Often, I said nasty things to them and tried to control them. It was my only outlet for venting my pent-up aggression and sadness that I really didn't know how to deal with on my own. I spent a lot of evenings in my bedroom crying. I needed help but felt like nobody understood me, and they were too quick to tell me how I was wrong for whatever I had said or done that day.

My main problem was that nobody asked me why I behaved that way. I just wanted someone to ask. I was constantly told by adults to cheer up, or that I was so stroppy, or to stop being a baby. They often commented, 'Oh, she's crying again,' yet nobody asked me why I was doing these things.

It's easy to look back now and say that all I had to do was tell them I was being abused, and I was unable to deal with the emotional trauma that would come from that. It's also easy to say I should have asked someone to help me understand how to process and regulate the feelings so I wouldn't continue to think it was my fault or that I deserved it because I was a bad person who didn't deserve nice things. I also felt as if I wasn't allowed to cry because, apparently, I needed to just 'be good' (although I was clearly not a good person, so how could I be good?), and so the cycle continued.

I vaguely remember boys a little older than me (ten years and older) trying to touch and kiss me; I thought it was normal. As an adult, it's frightening to think that this stuff is happening to young children.

One boy from a rough, local family once told me that I couldn't play with him unless I kissed him. I didn't want to kiss him because he was ugly and smelly, and he wasn't very nice to anyone. He threatened to throw me into the ditch, so I just left and never got to play outside in the sun. It was becoming commonplace to have males wanting to touch me, and it reinforced my feeling of being unsafe. It also contributed to my anger, which I expressed in my daily life.

Reflecting on these experiences in my early, most impressionable years makes me realise just how important it is to actually speak with children and really listen to what they tell you. There's always a reason people act out, and it's not just because they are 'badly behaved'—it doesn't come from nowhere. As children, we may not be cognitively developed, but we can still feel when we're frightened, or we don't like something. It's frustrating and damaging to have adults tell you who you are, what you are, and how you should feel. This was the second thing that exacerbated my feelings of disempowerment, worthlessness and not being good enough. From the daily teasing and criticism from my dad and brothers to the lack of support when I cried because of it, to the lectures from adults telling me what type of person I was, I quickly developed the belief that my feelings weren't valid, and I was not a nice person. When you're told something every day, you believe it to be the truth. Words are powerful, and I didn't have the mental or emotional intelligence back then to distinguish between my truth and someone else's perception of me.

Abraham Hicks[1] says that, over time, with enough pressure from those surrounding us, who seem convinced that their way is more valid (and righter) than our way, we slowly

---

[1] An American author and speaker on the subject of the Law of Attraction.

release our determination to guide our own lives. Sometimes, it is easier to adapt to others' ideas of what is best for us rather than figure it out ourselves. People always advise or judge you based on their own perceptions and levels of emotional intelligence. In allowing these people to determine who you are and how you should live your life, you end up giving away your freedom to create.

A child wouldn't understand this, but it's important that we, as adults, learn it to ensure we do not suppress children from speaking their truths and feeling safe to be their authentic, creative selves.

CHAPTER 3

Crying out Unheard

Already feeling ashamed and disgusting, I was also massively insecure about my body. I actually began hating the summer because it meant wearing fewer clothes. The hatred and fear were more significantly felt throughout my teenage years. The idea of showing off my ugly body filled me with the most overwhelming anxiety. After years of being told I was ugly, I developed round shoulders from dropping my head down and staring at the floor. Holding my head up for people to see my face felt like total exposure that led to fear and danger, and I just couldn't handle it. I felt so unsafe being seen; I just wanted to hide away in my bedroom and slip into my imagination. However, in doing this, I got picked on by my family for not having any friends and staying in my room all the time. The trouble was that I couldn't identify with any of my peers because I carried this secret that was eroding me from the inside and damaging my perspective of life. I couldn't articulate the pain I felt, and I could only react with aggression. Even when the girls at school were being nice to me, I was defensive because I didn't believe I deserved the kindness, and therefore, I couldn't understand why anyone wanted to be kind to me. I didn't get along with girls so much growing up, mainly because I didn't want to be one. I wanted to be a boy because I believed they didn't get touched like I did (although now I know that's not the case).

I began dressing like a boy, in tracksuit bottoms and baggy T-shirts. My mum always tried to dress me like a girl, and I bloody hated it! It just felt too dangerous to wear pretty dresses, as I felt way more vulnerable and exposed. I really felt I stood out compared to my brothers, who didn't have to wear the same. They weren't being abused, so it felt really unfair (I adopted this constant feeling of 'unfairness' and carried it, along with the other baggage of emotions, into my future relationships). I thought that if I could dress and act like a boy, then boys wouldn't want to touch me anymore. Also, I thought I was so ugly that who would want to see my horrible body, the freckles on my face, my big chin, my horrible teeth and my hunched back? What was there to dress up and show off?

As I got to my teenage years, this became increasingly difficult. My female peers dressed feminine and wore make-up while I was still covered head-to-toe in sports gear. The summer holidays were horrendous. I was so hot, but I didn't dare wear a dress or anything that would show off my body. I was disgusting and would probably look like a tart, asking for trouble from men. My back had become significantly more bowed during my teenage years, especially once I started growing boobs. Those things needed hiding away! I purposely pulled my shoulders forward so nobody would see my boobs poking through my T-shirt. Obviously, that didn't conceal my boobs and only resulted in my having a more significantly bowed upper back.

I became friends with a pretty blonde girl who constantly told me that boys preferred blondes and that blondes were on TV because they were sexier than brunettes. Alongside my daily taunts of being called 'ugly', I started to despise blonde women and was determined to remain brunette, going to the extreme of dying my hair jet black (which did NOT compliment my skin tone at all!). My uncle started calling me Marilyn Manson because my hair was dark, and my skin was so pale. It didn't help that I wore black eyeliner to make my eyes appear smaller, as I hated the size of them, and I wore dark clothes as I thought bright colours would make me stand out in a crowd.

After more years of looking as if I'd just crawled out of a grave, I decided to try the blonde look, believing it would ease my insecurities—after all, blondes had more fun, right? Wrong. Nothing bloody changed other than that I was going to the salon more frequently to get my roots touched up. It's amazing how we put so much emphasis on something external to ourselves and assume our troubles will be over if we conform to that idea, when in actuality, the resolution of our troubles is deep within us and can't be purchased.

So, all those years, I walked around hiding my body under baggy clothes and looking as if I had a severe vitamin

D deficiency whilst my female friends had begun to blossom. They all looked gorgeous (and they were all blonde). I was the same physically, unfortunately, but at least my personality had changed slightly: I was funny, and I made people laugh. I was mature for my age, so I was always the one friends came to for advice because I was reliable, loyal and dependable, all of the qualities the other girls did not possess. A slight whiff of dick, and those girls would drop you faster than they could drop their knickers. This further cemented my feelings of rejection and abandonment that I had first internalised at five years old. It was hard for me to feel safe enough to open up to anyone, and I couldn't do it with those 'friends' because I knew that, at any moment, I'd be ditched for some dick. Yet, as soon as it went sour with a guy, guess who was the first person they came crying to? Moi, apparently. Then, the whole pattern of behaviour happened again.

I actually started to feel more secure around my male friends because they never ditched me to get laid. They didn't need to because they still valued time with their friends despite the fact they had girlfriends. Also, those guys never tried to touch me, and of course, they wouldn't because I was a pale, withered, hunchbacked skinny beanpole. I felt safe with them, knowing nobody was about to abuse me there, and that was where I wanted to stay.

In my teenage years, my dad left, giving my mum the ultimatum that he would stay if she moved us kids out of the house. This pushed my rejection and abandonment wounds to a deeper level. Of course, my mum refused to do this. Who wanted to remain with a man who suggested that? Although, there is a part of me that thinks he proposed this knowing she would say no, and therefore, he could manipulate this to his advantage and blame her for his leaving. Following his sudden departure, without explanation as to why he was even going, without even a goodbye, drugs took his place in my life.

I bloody loved my drugs! Ah, just being able to escape the world was incredible!

Most people danced and chatted crap when they were high; I just sat quietly, watching my friends have fun and just enjoying being free of all the emotional baggage I'd been carrying for so many years. Ah, man—it felt so good! In that state, people asked if I were okay because I was so withdrawn, but honestly, I was having an absolute ball!

But what goes up must come down, and boy, were my comedowns horrendous. I was fucking nasty! I raged! The rage was my real self. My authentic emotions coming back to life. This was most felt after I had been on a bender for a few days. Having so much relief from reality and feeling that freedom to come back into your body and having those dominant feelings appear again was the worst. It was just so overwhelming having to feel that again, and it made me really angry that I had to go back to it.

It was a wise idea to stay away from me when I was on a comedown! MDMA, cocaine and base became my tools for escaping my demons because, at the time, I was unaware that

I could heal my trauma in a healthy way, but just like when I was five, I didn't speak up and ask for help, so I never got it.

During my teenage years, there were a few boys I had sex with, but really, it was nothing to write home about, and quite literally, in this case, nothing to write about! They were all unfulfilling, empty experiences that left me feeling exploited and used. I felt the same feelings I had when the pervert had finished with me. This was a predominant feeling; one I had spent my whole life believing was 'normal'. I remember my friend's mum giving some awful advice once. She said, 'Sex is all about the man. You need to make sure he is getting the pleasure.' I believed this at the time because it already fitted in perfectly with my narrative surrounding men and intimacy. However, if I could go back in time and slap her around the face for talking such nonsense, I would!

I felt inferior and subservient to men. With this belief absorbing every fabric of my being and therefore, setting the standard for my life experiences, it was inevitable that I was only ever going to attract people and situations into my life that reflected my internal state of mind. Dr Joe Dispenza[2] says in his book, 'Breaking the Habit of Being Yourself', that we condition our bodies to live in the past. He says that our experiences can create emotional reactions, which then cause moods that may last hours or days. If we do not make a conscious choice to focus on new desired experiences, our

---

[2] Dispenza, J. (2012). *Breaking the Habit of Being Yourself: How to Lose Your Mind.* Hay House. Hicks, E. & Hicks, J. (2009). *Ask and it is Given: Learning to Manifest Your Deisres.* Hay House.

moods can turn into a habit or a behaviour over weeks or months. If we decide not to confront this and heal from it, it can become a personality trait over the years, where we have memorised our emotional reactions and stay stuck, living in the past. Dr Joe Dispenza also goes on to say that as events trigger the same chemical response as the original incident, your body may think it is re-experiencing the same event.

My subconscious was conditioned to believe that all intimate experiences would include abuse, shame, rejection, abandonment, and trauma. Therefore, this was what I unconsciously sought as it was the only thing familiar to me. At the time, I wasn't aware that these thoughts and memories were running the show. I believed that life was happening *to* me, not *for* me, and that I was a victim of it. I was operating with a victim-like mentality, and therefore, attracted experiences into my life that treated me as such.

I frequently attracted toxicity, but nothing would prepare me for the most significant, most toxic period in my life. That was when I met Callum.

CHAPTER 4

Dealers, Drugs and Depression

After scraping the bottom of the barrel with no self-respect for years, I met Callum, who was also at the bottom of the same barrel. Callum was a 30-year-old drug dealer who gave me drugs and had sex with me at the age of 17. This guy really did think he was the dog's bollocks. I mean, he most definitely wasn't, but then neither was I. I believed he had more than me—he had his own flat and a constant supply of drugs. This was the perfect combination for me as I wanted to run away and escape the demons inside my head, and I could hide out in his flat away from the people who knew me. I could also escape from myself using the drugs he supplied me with. Perfect.

Or so I thought.

This quickly turned into a relationship encompassing three years of lies, deceit, neglect, toxicity and eventually, depression. It really was bloody horrible, and this guy should be ashamed of himself for exploiting a young girl in order to make himself feel important, useful and wanted.

When I first met Callum, I was working in a local shop. He left his wallet in the shop one evening after I had served him. I didn't notice it on the counter until after he had left. I picked up the wallet. It felt thick, so I took a peek inside to see that it was filled with wads of £20 notes! My first thought was, 'This guy's a drug dealer,' there was so much money in there. It was more than was necessary to be carrying around. Most people who earned that amount of cash legitimately would have it in the bank. Realising that this was a lot of money to lose and remembering that this guy was always pleasant to me when he came into the shop, I decided to keep it safe for him until I saw him again.

At some point that evening, he came rushing into the shop with a face full of panic, eyes wide, asking if he had left his wallet there. I replied, 'Yes,' and pulled it out from underneath the counter to give back to him. He almost slumped over the counter with relief. He thanked me for my honesty and said he would take me out for a drink sometime as a way to say thank you. I was quite pleased with the idea and said yes to it.

How I wish now that I had just said, 'No, ta. Just give me one of those £20 notes, and we'll call it quits.'

I had already guessed he was a dealer, so to be sure, I asked a couple of people about him, and they confirmed my suspicions. I was also told that he was a loser, a waste of space, physically abusive to some of his previous girlfriends, and had a disturbing attraction to young girls (one of his ex-girlfriends had been 15, and he was 28 when they were together!). So, armed with this information, what did I do? I ignored it and went out for that drink.

I took comfort in the fact that this guy was more broken than I was, so I could put my energy into 'fixing' him and would, therefore, not have to think about or deal with my own issues. At the time, I was also going through an extremely uneventful, unfulfilling experience with another guy, who had recently been in trouble with the law for beating up his ex-girlfriend, but Callum was nicer to me, and he made me laugh, unlike the other one. I already had no self-respect, no boundaries and no idea how I deserved to be treated, so I took Callum up on his offer of a drink, thinking it was a good idea.

Things between Callum and I progressed very quickly (as was to be expected when two insecure individuals started to bond with one another). We both relied upon the other to provide us with the love and support we couldn't give to ourselves.

In his book, 'The Power of Now', Eckhart Tolle[3] describes how love is within us and not found externally, as society today believes. He goes on to explain how people will seek a relationship to cover up any unease they feel if they cannot be at ease with themselves when they are alone, and states;

"The unease will then reappear in some other form within the relationship, and you will probably hold your partner responsible for it.'

And this is exactly what happened. I blamed Callum for my downfall.

---

[3] Tolle, E. (1997). *The Power of Now: A Guide to Spiritual Enlightenment*. New World Library.

Our entire relationship was based around my making him feel better about his shit life and was always geared to what would benefit his needs. I realise it's easy to ask why I stuck around if he was such scum, but remember, he was a reflection of how I felt about myself. I thought I was scum and a shit person. I had thought this since I was five years old, ever since the pervert forced me into that frightening world that I should never have been exposed to. Of course, if I believed I was a good person who deserved a healthy relationship, then I would have run for the hills the moment Callum laid his eyes on me. Unfortunately, my self-hatred and severe lack of self-esteem found that loser to be my Prince Charming (gross, but true).

Because Callum was 30 and I was 17, I believed that despite his issues, he would be a good provider. He had his own place and more money than me. Although I had a job and made my own money, I certainly wasn't in a position of security. I was 17 years old, living at my mum's. I wasn't supposed to have a career and my own place, but as a teenager, you tend to desire these things.

Callum asked me to move in with him a short while after we started dating, and I accepted. His flat was nice but hectic. There was a constant stream of people coming and going, buying drugs from him. His phone was non-stop ringing, with people asking for drugs. There was always somebody who needed to crash on the sofa for a few days because they had fallen out with a partner or a parent and couldn't go home. It was so busy that we never had a moment of peace. We never sat down to have a conversation, and we never went out to do anything together.

It was pretty boring, really, but at least I could have my friends over, and we could take ecstasy and cocaine.

We didn't stay in that flat for very long because Callum got evicted. The landlord was (quite rightly) fed up with the neighbours complaining of the swarms of people going in and out of the house at all hours and the anti-social behaviour. Callum's landlord had previously warned that he would be evicted if he allowed this to continue, but he didn't care; he didn't listen, and therefore, he was served his notice to leave. Of course, he blamed it on the landlord and the neighbours and not at all on himself. Little did I know it at the time, but that was the beginning of a pattern. We moved six times in three years: three places we lived alone together, two places we rented a room in someone else's house and one time, we took up residence in his mum's living room. There was just never any security or stability.

When I got with Callum, I didn't realise that he was a heroin addict. He knew he had this addiction before we got together, so he knew all the problems that came with his addiction, but he still chose to ask me to be his girlfriend and subjected me to that life. I feel as if he tricked me into that life, knowing I wouldn't have gone with him had I known of his addiction beforehand. Sometimes, I feel resentment at this. I have worked on it and generally am at peace with that part of my life now, but sometimes, a lingering feeling manifests itself when I relive that time.

I have since learnt about being the 'watcher' and not the 'reactor' to feelings, so, I watch and notice the resentment without judgement and allow it to leave without reacting to its presence. I can do this now, but back then, I wasn't aware of how to release the negative energy from my body, so I became reactive to my feelings instead, and this was often aggressive.

Once you know how to release the negative feelings from your body, and you experience a significant shift in your body and your perspective, you will want to do this every day. It's a simple technique that can be done anywhere.

When you feel a negative emotion, don't label it. Instead, acknowledge it's there and breathe through it. Continue to breathe, and eventually, you will feel it move its way up slowly from your stomach area (solar plexus) into your chest (heart centre), all the way to the top of your head (crown) and release. When you check back in with your body after doing this exercise, you will notice that the feeling you had minutes before has lost all of its power and grip over you. You have just released stuck energy and freed your body up to allow in lighter, more positive energy and/or feelings.

In the early days of our relationship, I noticed that Callum spent a lot of time in the bathroom. The excuses started with him having a 'dicky tummy'. Then, after a few weeks, he could no longer use the same story as I was close to calling his GP, so he switched it to needing frequent wees or having a bath. The bath narrative stopped the moment I discovered the bath was bone dry when he left the bathroom. When I asked why the bath was dry, he was adamant that he had had a bath and dried the tub after he got out (said no one ever), but addicts lie about literally everything, no matter how dumb it sounds.

Around this time, Callum had a weird mate who came over frequently who also used the bathroom for long periods of time; he was another person who couldn't, apparently, control his bowels. Then, the rumours around town began to circulate that Callum was using heroin. I confronted him, but he denied it, of course. One morning, I was in a café when three local heroin users asked if I was going out with Callum. When I said yes, they looked at each other and turned away from me. I now know it was because they knew Callum was using, and I didn't have a clue at the time.

Callum eventually told me the truth, but only because his friend gave him an ultimatum and said he would tell me himself if Callum didn't. By then, I had become so suspicious that I constantly asked people if Callum was on the gear.

My more evolved, grown self cannot fathom why I chose to stay with him, but my broken, hated self kept me there. I believed I could save him from his misery, and that would be a distraction from having to deal with mine. In doing this, I could also take on the role of the important, better one of the two of us. I had never felt superior to anyone in my life, so it felt good to take on this position when I was with Callum. Whichever way you look at it, we used each other and exploited the other's issues and vulnerability to make ourselves feel good.

When I first got with Callum, I was already at college doing business studies, for no particular reason other than I didn't know what I wanted to do in life, and my mum kept on at me to go to college after leaving school to gain further qualifications as my GCSE results were pretty crap. That's not because I didn't have the ability to do well in my exams; it was because I lacked confidence and had no drive or ambition to try to succeed.

I didn't enjoy college. I couldn't concentrate in class because I was tired all the time. I was quite unhealthy back then. I wasn't eating properly, and I was doing so many drugs over the weekend and drinking during the week. This, combined with my constant state of anxiety, took a huge toll on my body. I was fatigued all the time. My eyelids got heavy during the classes I attended, and I just couldn't get up and out of bed for the others. I was exhausted from the moment I opened my eyes, and I longed for it to be bedtime again. I kept a diary around that time, which I wish I had, but unfortunately, I threw it away. I didn't value or care about my feelings enough to read what I had written and take notice of what my inner self and/or my intuition was trying to tell me. I dismissed and discarded my diaries, thereby dismissing and discarding my feelings and subsequently creating a pattern of how I allowed other people to treat me going forward.

I was on the brink of quitting college only months from the completion date because I felt so shit and had no energy to concentrate on anything. I only remained and passed that course because my friend, Marie, had noticed my sharp decline, so she drove to my place and forced me to get up to go to college. She also helped me do my coursework as I didn't have a clue what was going on. Again, like my GCSEs, it was not because I wasn't capable of getting good grades—it was because I lacked the confidence and motivation to even try. Marie really did drag me through those remaining months at college, ensuring I passed the course, and she has been by my side ever since. So, for that, I am truly grateful.

Around this period, Callum sent me into a bit of a spin. He had trouble deciding if he wanted to remain with me or go back to his ex (another 17-year-old). This 30-year-old man had difficulty choosing which 17-year-old he wanted to make his 'ride-or-die'. Absolute joker.

Anyway, it turned out that I was the 'lucky one'. I don't know what's worse: being chosen by the disgusting loser or being rejected by him. Obviously, at the time, I thought I was the cat who had got the cream. Instead, I was the dog who was being sent to the rescue centre to live out the next three years in a cage. The other girl had made a lucky escape. I don't know what happened to her, but I did, unfortunately, come across some photos of her in Callum's flat. They were of her and Callum naked in bed, and one of her giving him oral sex. She was 16 at the time, and he was 29, and he had held onto the photos. This was before camera phones, so the photos had been taken on a disposable camera, and he had kept them, along with the negatives. The girl was barely out of school.

I don't mind an age gap—in fact, I like older men—but Callum had a habit of plucking girls fresh out of school.

After spending some time renting a room in Callum's friend's house, we found a flat and moved in, but it wasn't too long before Callum's grim mates started coming over. There were two brothers I remember in particular because they were both in their mid-30s, and their girlfriends were 14 and 15. I seemed to be surrounded by men who exploited young, vulnerable girls. This was the life I was familiar with, and it appeared normal to me. I understood that these girls needed someone to look after them, just as I did, and I knew that was why we were with those men. I can see now that those guys needed more help than we did.

I really did experience the worst side of society being with him. The people coming over to our house, either to buy drugs from him or to take heroin with him, consisted of paedophiles, burglars, rapists, woman beaters and addicts. Most addicts just need some help in life. Those people, I didn't mind sitting on my sofa. It was the others I hated having around, but I accepted that it was what I deserved in life.

After some months at that flat, we moved into a house across the street. With both of us paying the rent and bills, we could afford to live in a bigger place. It was so modern and clean, and I really loved it. Callum had made the decision to give up the heroin and go cold turkey. The first night of going cold turkey was horrendous. His temper was awful. He kept storming around the place, throwing things, screaming at me to get him heroin, threatening to kill himself, and at one point, throwing sharp kitchen knives at the wall. All I could do was follow him around to make sure he didn't harm himself and remain calm when he shouted at me. This went on all through the night. I had to call his mum to come and help me because I was so tired and couldn't keep following him around, calming him down and clearing up any mess he made after throwing things.

When his mum came over, I had a couple of hours of sleep, and then, when I woke, she went to sleep. We had to take turns to watch that he didn't hurt himself or go out to buy heroin. I was terrified. It was a really horrible and eye-opening experience. It was at that point I realised that Callum was extremely vulnerable, and I needed to look after him. What I witnessed was a frightening reminder of the power that poisonous drugs had on someone, and I now understood why many people fail to become free of its evil grip.

CHAPTER 5

Silent Battles, Empty Echoes

My empathy for Callum deepened after seeing his reaction to the withdrawal, and I began treating him with kid gloves for fear of him having a bad day and relapsing. He remained clean for just a few days before going back to it. After what I had witnessed when he went cold turkey, I softened to the idea of him being back on the gear because I had a front-row seat to the physical pain he was in. When he confessed he was back on it, I didn't shout or kick off and cause him any problems. I empathised with him, and unfortunately, I believe this enabled him to continue using.

Almost immediately after this experience, I began taking a dominant role with Callum. This guy required so much looking after; it was unreal. Although Callum had a mum, he told me she'd been neglectful when he was a child, and he was put into the care system. I believe I became the mother he never had in the sense that I always had to look after him and help him out of trouble. He always sought attention and validation. He literally couldn't do anything for himself and relied on me for everything. I cooked, cleaned, paid the bills, paid the rent, arranged for him to go back to college (which he dropped out of after a couple of lessons), arranged for him to get a job (which he lost due to his drug use) and I fought his battles for him. He was always falling out with people because he didn't have any genuine friends, only people who bought drugs from him or who wanted to sit in our house and take them.

Callum did not support me with anything. I carried him on my back throughout our relationship. I was familiar with not being supported, so I didn't know any different and continued to give to him.

When we discovered someone had broken into our house, he asked me to go and confront the person he believed to have done it on his behalf because he was too scared to do it himself. We came home one evening to find the front door ajar, and his X-Box had been stolen. He suspected it had been the next-door neighbour, so he asked me to go over to confront him, which I did. It turned out it wasn't the neighbour but one of Callum's so-called 'friends'. We found this out because the thief told my friend, who then told me. My friend and I got together to get the X-Box back from the pawn shop, and Callum didn't do anything to help, even though it was his computer.

Another demonstration of Callum's lack of support for me came when we were in Italy. A man tried to rob me by pulling at my handbag, and Callum just walked away. I stood there, pulling back and forth with the man who said I owed him money because he'd tied a bit of cheap string around my wrist and attempted to call it a bracelet. I wasn't about to pay ten Euros for that crap, so he grabbed my handbag. Callum saw everything from the moment the guy approached me right up to my pulling away from him, clutching tightly onto my handbag, and his response was to turn his back and walk away from me. Another man came over and shouted at me in Italian, pointing his finger at my face (I think the two were working together). It caused quite a scene, and someone must have alerted the police as two officers suddenly appeared and got the men away from me. I was fuming with Callum for having left me, and it was then I realised that he was never going to support me in anything, but I also believed that I didn't deserve anyone's support. I hadn't had it in my life before, so why would I get it now?

The most sobering example of Callum's willingness not to consider me in anything came when his heroin dealer stormed into the house and threatened Callum because he had bought drugs from another dealer. This guy was pure evil. He was a monster of a man, six-foot-five with steroid-induced muscles, no neck and a vile temper. He was known to carry knives, so when he reached into the back pocket of his jeans after shouting at Callum for buying from someone else, my body froze with fear. He stood in the doorway so neither of us could get away from him. Luckily, as soon as he reached for the back pocket of his jeans, he changed his personality, exhaled, slumped on the sofa and put his head in his hands. He apologised for bursting through the door as he had and frightening Callum (though he didn't apologise to me).

I was already terrified of the man because I knew he regularly beat his girlfriend and made threats to kill her. I knew he had hit one of his customer's girlfriends as a message for the guy to hurry up and pay the money he owed him. I told Callum not to get into trouble with that dealer because I would be the one punished by him as a warning. I genuinely thought the guy was going to pull a knife out on me because Callum had pissed him off.

I felt betrayed by him again, but I still didn't have the awareness to recognise that this was a pattern, and he would continue to betray me and put me in danger unless I did something to change it.

This episode with the dealer instigated Callum to have some dodgy guys come over to discuss a retaliation. I pleaded with him not to do it because he would make the situation worse, but he went ahead anyway. Of course.

There were three guys hunched over the coffee table in my living room, quietly talking about what they were going to do to the dealer. I busied myself in the kitchen because I didn't want to be a part of anything that was about to happen. After all, it was not my problem. It was the fault of Callum and his drug use.

During the meeting, it was suggested that I could potentially be followed, kidnapped, held and beaten up by the dealer and his associates. By that point, I no longer went out because I felt I was too disgusting to be seen in public, so I wasn't too concerned about those things ever happening. I also knew there would be no point in the dealer doing anything because Callum was so broke, he couldn't pay up to get me back. He also didn't care about my safety. He'd left me when the two guys in Italy had tried to rob me, and he'd got on the wrong side of this meathead of a dealer, knowing he had the potential to attack the girlfriends of whoever pissed him off.

I'm not completely clear on how this was resolved in the end. I believe the dealer's competitor, the one Callum had been buying from, got wind of this and threatened the meathead so he'd leave me and Callum alone. It was all very political and territorial, and quite frankly, had nothing to do with me. The competitor was also a monster of a man who had broken both of his girlfriend's arms, but at least he was always really kind to me whenever he came over.

After just a few months of living in this new house, we got evicted. The police raided the house following a tip-off that Callum was dealing. It was local knowledge that Callum was a dealer, and he was well-known to the police, so it was only a matter of time before they arrived. Thankfully for me, the police first kicked in the door of our previous place across the road, causing quite a scene and giving me time to pack some things and get out of there before they came through our door. The police managed to get another warrant and raid our new house after I had left. They didn't find drugs in the house, but had they searched the flower bed opposite the kitchen window; they would have found everything they needed.

We were lucky to get away with it, and I told Callum I didn't want to go through it again. He agreed to stop dealing, and I believed him until a few weeks later, when we returned from visiting friends in India. Someone had given Callum some cannabis seeds, and he couldn't resist the temptation to take them back to England to grow, bag up and sell. I didn't realise he had this, so when we were pulled aside at Heathrow Airport to have our suitcases searched, I didn't feel the need to panic. I remember feeling a little apprehensive when the lady searched through all my things, but I turned around and saw Callum standing next to me, smiling, and it made me feel a bit better. It wasn't until we had left the airport that he told me he had hidden the drugs in my bag. I was fuming! That devious asshole had put it in my luggage and not his! I'm glad I didn't know it was there because my nerves would have got the better of me, and the staff member would have known for sure that I was attempting to hide something. I was so mad at him, yet despite all he had done to me, I still didn't leave him. My mindset still made me believe that I didn't deserve better than that. What he did there was to demonstrate to me that he would always put me in the firing line as long as he benefitted from it. He wanted to take the drugs home, and he wanted to sell them, so he should have put them in his luggage. Instead, he chose to hide them in my bag without my knowing and stood next to me, smiling as my bag was being searched. I wish I had left him at that point, but I didn't like or respect myself enough to do it. Being the victim had become a part of my DNA, so I expected to be treated in such a way.

We went back to our new home together, which was a room in someone else's house, and continued our toxic relationship. We remained at that house for a little while before getting evicted again, and then we moved into Callum's mums.

Living at his mum's was awful. She was always arguing with Callum's stepdad, constantly shouting at him for the slightest thing. Callum had pre-warned me that his mum was a hypochondriac, and he was absolutely right. She complained every day about how ill she was. The atmosphere in the house was extremely negative, and it began to affect my already vulnerable mental health.

The house had two reception rooms on the ground floor, one at the back—used as a living room, and one at the front—used for storage. There was a sofa in there but no TV as it wasn't used. This was the room Callum and I moved into. We put a blow-up bed on the floor. It didn't take long before Callum's mum began complaining and dropping hints that she wanted her front room back. We were both paying rent to sleep on the floor of that unused room, and we kept out of her way as best we could, but it still wasn't good enough. She made such a big deal about how she was doing us a favour, but we were homeless, and Callum was her son—why wouldn't she want to help us? In addition to that, we had paid to be there, bought our own food and cleaned up after ourselves. It's a deeply shameful feeling when you know you are not welcome in someone's house, and you know you are a burden to them, but you literally have nowhere else to go. In hindsight,

I could have gone back to my mum's, where I would have been welcomed, and I would have had a bed, free of charge until I was earning enough money to pay rent or move out to my own place, but I felt that Callum was so low and vulnerable, and I knew he wanted to be with his mum because he craved her love and approval, so I remained by his side.

By that point, Callum had been out of work for some time as his drug use made it difficult for him to hold down a job. We couldn't afford to rent a place on my wages alone, especially now that I was paying rent to his mum to sleep on the floor, so we contacted the council to be put on the housing list. We were put at the bottom of the list because we had somewhere to stay, so we weren't technically homeless. Callum, his family and I all thought this was really unfair, and we hated the Council for letting us down.

Looking back, I now agree with the council. Why should they give us accommodation? because Callum couldn't sort out his shit? Why should they give us accommodation? Because Callum's mum wanted her front room back (which she doesn't use)? I was stuck in a victim-like mentality where I believed everyone and everything was out to get me, and the more I thought about it, the more I attracted experiences to make me feel even further like a victim.

It was taking far too long to move up the housing list, and Callum's mum was getting more and more stressed by our presence. Callum's drug use had taken a firm grip over his life, controlling every aspect of it, and I was going insane. I wanted to help Callum. I wanted to heal him, and I wanted to fix him, but while I was doing that and putting him first, I wasn't helping, healing, or fixing myself. Without realising it, my mental health was in significant decline, and I was creating a life of misery for myself. My self-esteem was in the gutter. I felt degraded, ashamed, embarrassed, and trapped. We were clearly not wanted in that house, but we couldn't leave until we had somewhere else to go.

I often sat on the blow-up bed on the floor and stared into space. I wasn't looking at anything in particular; I was just drowning in a pit of negative thoughts. I could sit there for hours, thinking about how disgusting I was, how I wasn't good for anything and how I was a shit loser that didn't deserve good things happening to me.

When you give your attention to something, your body responds accordingly to that thought. Each time you focus on the thought, it becomes easier for your body to respond to it. Then, when you consistently focus on it again and again and have repeated this line of thought long enough, it becomes a belief. With these negative thoughts having become my beliefs, the Law of Attraction accepted them as my point of attraction and brought all things matching my thoughts to me. Esther Hicks[4] says in her book 'Ask and it is Given: Learning to Manifest Your Desires' that 'Anything you give your attention to, will become your "truth". Your life, and everyone else's too, is but a reflection of the predominance of your thoughts.'

---

[4] Hicks & Hicks, 2009

This was how I created my miserable existence, by focusing upon how it was a miserable existence and believing it was what I deserved. I was not aware of the Law of Attraction back then, so I was not capable of making the decision to direct my thoughts, deliberately choosing to redirect them to another point of attraction. I was also unaware that in order for something in my life to change, I had to change something. I believed that life happened to me and not for me. I believed I was a victim, and I had no control over my life, and I simply sat waiting for something external to transform my life.

During that time, I began ignoring my friends' phone calls or making excuses not to meet them. I couldn't face people seeing the shit person I had become. I had this constant, overwhelming, heavy feeling of anxiety swirling around in my stomach. I felt my shoulders slumping forwards more than they already did, and I hung my head lower than usual. I felt too ashamed of myself to stand up straight and be seen. I was disgusting.

During the time spent staring into space, I often asked myself, 'How did my life turn out like this?' I felt so powerless and out of control. I felt hopeless, asking myself why this had happened to me, feeling as if I were being punished and that nothing good would ever happen to me.

One night, my friend Marie eventually got me to go out. I felt resentful about it because I didn't own any nice clothes, and no matter what I wore, I looked ugly in it. I couldn't walk in heels because I was too tall, I couldn't wear tight trousers because my legs were too skinny, and I had no ass, and I couldn't wear a tight top because of my hunchback. I got so angry trying on all those clothes because I felt hideous in everything.

Marie came to pick me up from Callum's mums, so I didn't have much choice to back out, and we went into town, and I actually ended up having a really good time! Just being away from Callum and our living environment was so refreshing. I was away from conflict, arguing and negative talk. It was such a relief, and I enjoyed watching people my age have fun in the bars. It reminded me that this was what I should be doing. I was 19 at the time depressed, looking after my heroin-addicted 32-year-old boyfriend, sleeping on his mum's front room floor. It wasn't the life I wanted or needed. I wanted to be out having fun and being carefree like Marie and all the other people around me in the bar. I wanted to leave Callum, I really did, but the guilt kept me with him alongside the negative self-belief. I felt as if I couldn't leave him until he was clean. If I could just get him clean, if I could just know he was okay, then I could leave him. That was my plan, but I didn't have £4,000 to put him through rehab. I couldn't even afford to put down a deposit to rent a home for us.

I stayed over at Marie's that night, and I slept so well in the bed on a mattress. It felt so good to have a cooked breakfast in the morning, too. I felt wonderful and refreshed because for a few hours, I got to be someone else. I got to be a 19-year-old, out with her friend, having fun.

When it was time for Marie to take me back, I had this overwhelming feeling of anxiety blow up in my stomach, and I felt a deep sense of sadness as if I wanted to scream out, 'Please don't take me back there!' The familiar feelings I had as a child when the perv was touching me resurfaced, and I wanted to cry out to Marie, 'But you don't understand what's happening to me!' I wanted to hide away and not be seen.

I should have spoken up and told Marie (or anyone in my life) how I felt and asked for their help to leave Callum, but, just like when I was five, I didn't say anything, and I went back to that house without saying a word, holding back my tears.

As soon as I entered the house, Callum's stepdad pulled me aside and said that Callum had tried to commit suicide the night before. I was in shock! His family had warned me that he was prone to threatening suicide, but I had never seen him attempt it before. I was told that he never went through with it, as each time he told someone what he was doing, he gave them time to talk him out of it. It was essentially a cry for help. This time around, he had written his mum a note that he had taken a load of pills, and she would find him dead in the bathroom. Either his mum or his stepdad found the note and rushed to the unlocked bathroom, got him out and took him to the hospital.

Upon hearing this, I knew he was in much deeper trouble than I had initially anticipated, and my desire to help accelerated. I pushed aside my feelings of wanting to be a 19-year-old and have fun with people my age, and I doubled down on taking care of him, going out of my way to ensure he was okay and that he would never attempt it again.

Putting even more of my focus and energy into him was exhausting because he required so much looking after. He was deeply insecure and craved so much attention and ego-stroking. He also frequently fell out with people, so he needed me to vent to or resolve the problems on his behalf. He always needed money for drugs, and he often begged me for it, and if I didn't give him any, he just stole it.

I found out that Callum was stealing money from my bank account and had been doing so for months. It was the odd £10 or £20 a few times a week. I wasn't reading my bank statements, so I didn't pick up on it for a long time. When I went to draw cash out one day, I saw I had a lot less in there than I should have. All of my bank statements were still in unopened envelopes, piled up on the side. I went back through six months' worth of bank statements I had and calculated that he had stolen £960 from me. He initially said it was me who had spent it, and I just hadn't realised how much I had been spending. It was only when I pointed out to him that there were days when money was withdrawn while I was doing a 12-hour shift at work that he admitted he had been taking my bank card and stealing my money.

Later on, after I had left him, he used that money to bribe me into going back to him, but the money meant nothing to me after I had left him, so I said he could keep it.

Callum complained to me all the time that he wasn't doing anything with his life, so I helped him enrol in a night class at the local college to help him learn a trade. He did two lessons, then quit. I was exhausted with him. Nothing I said or did was good enough to help him. I slowly went mute. I just sat there like an empty shell, saying nothing while he told me about his latest problem he needed help with. His problems, along with the atmosphere at his mum's, made me desperate to leave the house. After no luck on the council's housing list and with some money I had saved, we eventually found somewhere to live, and I naively thought it would be the end of our problems. It was an annexe at the back of a shop in our local town. It was tiny, dark, cold and mouldy, but at least it got us off of Callum's mum's front room floor. This was such great news, and I was so relieved.

However, the annexe was a genuine hole. When you walked through the front door, you immediately entered a tiny kitchen with no windows or ventilation. To the right of the kitchen there was a doorway to the living room. The living room was very narrow, but it had enough space for a two-seater sofa, a table and a television. From the living room, you entered the bedroom, which had a tiny shower room in the corner, kind of like a really shit ensuite. The bedroom had a very small window, which was incapable of letting much light in, but any light that did come in only reached a few feet; the bedroom was so dark and dingy. During the day, I had to switch on the light to see. It was like a bat cave in there. Not only was the annexe dark and mouldy, but it was bloody freezing, too! The landlord, who lived above the shop and worked in it, had control of the central heating system. Therefore, we only got heating when he put it on for himself. I struggled getting up for work in the mornings because it was so cold I had to change my clothes underneath the duvet cover. We had asked the landlord numerous times to put the heating on earlier for me, but he kept refusing, saying he would be too hot at that time. I had no clue about tenants' rights back then, nor did I have the mental ability to start researching the legalities of landlords' responsibilities. Had I done that, I would have discovered that legally, tenants must have control over the heating system at all times, but back then, my mind didn't stretch any further than what was happening in front of me there and then. Plus, I was still in a victim mentality, where nothing good ever happened to me, so I deserved to live in the freezing conditions.

Due to the freezing temperatures, darkness and lack of ventilation, we had severe black mould that began creeping up from behind the paintwork and started growing on our clothes. I frequently washed our clothes to get the mould off, and it cost me a fortune to run the washing machine. We had an old-fashioned electric meter where you needed to put a pound coin in to get it running, and I watched the dial spin around ridiculously fast when the washing machine was on. It was gut-wrenching, as we didn't have money to waste like that. Callum received around £350 a month in housing benefits, but he was spending the whole lot on heroin. I paid the rent, the electric and the food. The mould was so bad that my clothes smelt. I became ashamed whenever I went out because my clothes and hair smelt so strongly of dampness. It was horrible. No matter how much I washed the mould off the walls or my clothes, it just kept coming back. The walls were rotten through and through. The annexe was fit for a garage, not for a home.

After a couple of months of existing there, the bedclothes became damp. Again, I was always washing and changing them, but the bedroom was so damp and cold that the bedclothes would become almost wet from the moisture in the air. It was horrible to sleep in as I knew I was breathing in mould toxins all night.

If I wasn't breathing in mould, I was breathing in nicotine. I smoked, but Callum was terrible. He chain-smoked roll-ups, and he always had one hanging out the corner of his mouth, even after it had gone out.

I had been with Callum for three years, and my mental and physical health had spiralled so fast downhill. My days consisted of going to work, going home to sit on the sofa and smoke roll-ups and staring at the television (but not actually watching it) whilst Callum took heroin and passed out next to me. Sometimes, I would come home from work, the sun would be shining, and Callum would be sitting in the dark with all the blinds closed, taking heroin with his mates in the living room. It was horrible, and I hated going home, knowing I'd be welcomed by this.

Although we were in a one-bed flat, I wouldn't allow Callum into the bed for the last year of our relationship because he disgusted me, and I hated him so much that I couldn't stand him touching me. In addition to my resentment towards him, I didn't want to have sex with him in case he gave me HIV. I had gone for a blood test to make sure he hadn't given it to me from sharing needles. I was given the all-clear, but having sex with him was not worth the risk.

I was 20 by this point and feeling a world of stress. I was so unhealthy, and my spirit was slowly dying inside me. My life was shit. I had become a shell. I had no personality. I had become a provider, protector, carer and housekeeper all in one. I started to really resent Callum and became very bitter at everything and everyone. I hated myself, I hated life and I definitely hated Callum. I blamed him for dragging me down to his level. I blamed him for stripping me of my personality, finances and health. I didn't understand that if I took responsibility for my own actions and made the decision to leave him, then my problems would be over. Instead, I let myself consistently focus on the bad things and allowed them to control me rather than do something about them. Without realising it, my point of attraction was still focused on the negative aspects, and therefore, I continued to create more of the same.

That time of my life was the unhealthiest I have ever been. I don't know what was worse: my mental or physical health. My hair was brittle; it snapped off easily and wouldn't grow. When I was a child, I had long, lovely hair. During my time with Callum, I cut it short, and it just didn't grow back. It was too weak when I wasn't taking care of myself. My skin was grey, my face was drawn in and I had dark circles under my eyes. I had always been skinny, but now I had lost even more weight through stress and loss of appetite.

Because of my decline, I could no longer work. I struggled to get through the days. I was working in a nursing home at the time. The work was so demanding, physically and mentally, and I wasn't working well in either of those areas. I wasn't eating or sleeping properly, and my mind never gave me a break from fearful, negative thoughts. I began having panic attacks at work, and I couldn't keep up with the job because I was so drained from the inside out. I eventually signed off of work because of anxiety. I didn't know at the time that the constant feeling I had was called anxiety. I just knew I needed help, so I went to the doctors to get it.

It was there, with the doctor, that I broke down and told her about the sexual abuse from the perv. She advised me that I was feeling anxiety and that she would sign me off work. However, she was not at all helpful about the sexual abuse and certainly didn't signpost me to anyone. It was my first attempt at speaking out about the abuse and asking for help, and I felt really let down by that doctor. I felt as if I was being silenced. I'm sure the doctor didn't intend for that to happen, but my state of mind was so negative and fragile that I perceived everyone as being out to cause me harm somehow. As I didn't get the help I so desperately needed, I continued to suppress those feelings and became an empty shell.

Abraham Hicks[5] says that even empty feelings tell you something important and compares it to the fuel gauge in a car that indicates when the tank is empty. You receive this

---
[5] Hicks & Hicks, 2009

information and go to fill up the tank—doing nothing about it won't solve the problem. Feeling empty is a sign your thoughts are not taking you in the direction you desire to go, so you must do something about it. We are to follow our bliss, and in doing so, we eventually align with our desired outcomes, but when you are in negative circumstances—as I was—bliss seems impossible, and the Law of Attraction would not allow me to make an energetic shift to a different feeling (or vibration, as they describe it). I could not have jumped energetically in the same way that you can't tune your radio to 101FM and hear a song being played on 444AM.

So, with an empty tank and doing nothing about it, my mental health spiralled even further. I went for days without showering or brushing my teeth. I spent most of the day in bed, and sometimes, wouldn't even get up and dressed. I often cried as soon as I woke up because I couldn't stand the pain of being awake and living that shit life. I literally had nothing left to give. I didn't want to talk; I just wanted to cry, go to sleep and not wake up. I hated Callum, myself and my life so much.

It was such a stressful time, and I didn't feel safe in my home, my body or my mind. I hated that guy and the trouble he bought to my life. I wanted out, but I had got myself into such a pit that I didn't know how to escape, and I certainly couldn't see any light at the end of the tunnel. I was sad, I was grieving, I was deep in sorrow, and I couldn't believe that was my life.

CHAPTER 6
Breaking Away

When I was a child, I had an instinctive feeling there was a power much higher than us here on Earth, but I just didn't have the words to communicate what it was or the resources to research it. I now know that there is something else, and I understand that many people call it different things: Source, Universe, Creator, God. I lost my belief in this as I got older, as it was conditioned out of me to not believe in such 'rubbish' and 'hocus pocus'. During the final few months of my incredibly miserable existence with Callum, I began having strong dreams that I now understand were my inner self, trying to communicate with me in my sleep because my waking moments were heavily consumed with dark, suicidal thoughts. I'd already contemplated suicide when I was a teenager, wanting to hang from my school tie because I couldn't regulate my grubby emotions the pervert had impressed upon me. Now I was back to those feelings again, with another disgusting man who left me feeling grubby. The darker and more depressed my mind became, the stronger my dreams became. They were based all around my escaping from Callum and reaching a place where I felt safe, relieved, light and happy. I hadn't felt those feelings in my waking life for so long, and feeling them in my dreams was incredible, but then I woke up in that cold, dark, damp, mouldy flat and cried because I was awake in that life again.

In one of my dreams, I escaped from Callum and ran away to Australia! I was in Summer Bay from *Home and Away*, in the caravan park with Sally. I was so happy, but then I woke up, cried and the pattern of my existence continued into the following night.

After months of dreams in which I escaped from Callum, I had one final dream that changed the course of my life. My grandad came to me in that dream. I had ignored the messages from my inner self all those months, and now my grandad was taking over. My grandad died when I was six, so I have few memories of him, and I certainly wasn't thinking of him in my everyday life, but he came to me in my dream that night. I don't remember the words he said to me, but I absolutely remember how he made me feel. He was very firm with me and ordered me to leave Callum and go back to my mum's. That was the first time in years I woke up feeling a sense of confidence, knowing that I would leave Callum that day. It was also the first time in a very long time that I didn't cry or feel sad and depressed when I woke up. I just knew I was leaving Callum that morning despite the fact I knew he would threaten to kill himself again. After that realisation and newfound motivation coursing through my veins, I got dressed and walked out to the living room (where he slept). I remember that the sun was beaming outside, with a lovely blue sky, while he was sitting in the dark, smoking heroin.

I sat next to him on the sofa and told him I was leaving him. He stood up, threw an ashtray at the TV screen, shouted at me, and threatened to kill himself, but this time, there was a very clear choice for me: either he killed himself or I killed myself. For the first time in my life, I chose myself as the priority and walked out of that flat with nothing but the clothes on my back, my purse and my phone. All of my other belongings meant nothing to me anymore, so I left them there.

I moved back to my mum's that day. All of that confidence to leave him and move out had come from that one dream. I had spent three years of misery, longing to leave him and live a better life, but I couldn't do it. My thoughts had imprisoned me and convinced me I couldn't leave because it was what I deserved. The feeling that dream gave me was all I needed to walk out the door and step into a new life. I needed that intervention, and I'm so grateful it happened, as I know that if I had continued to live that way, I would have taken my own life.

In the weeks and months following the break-up, Callum tried to bribe me into getting my things back if I would go over to his and have a 'talk'. I simply told him to keep everything. It meant nothing to me anymore. I was away from him, and the sense of peace I felt was priceless and couldn't be compared to money or possessions. I was slowly getting my life back, and I no longer felt the anxiety in my stomach anymore. I had forgotten what that felt like, and I decided to go where I felt better—which was at Mum's, away from him.

Reflecting back on that journey, I can see how profound the shift in my energy was when I left Callum. A lot changed in my life incredibly quickly: I passed my driving test (I had failed twice when I was with Callum) and joined college to do an Access to Higher Education course with a view to study forensics. I took better care of my health, even investing in glasses to improve my eyesight, and I started to dress differently and began going out more.

I know the myriad of reasons why I remained with Callum for so long, and I've forgiven myself for staying. Callum, on the other hand, has never taken accountability for his part and certainly never apologised for any of his actions. All he ever did was justify, manipulate and blame others for his problems. That is why nothing could ever work or be resolved between us; it all got swept under the carpet, never to be seen or heard of again, just festering beneath the surface. I didn't feel safe to speak up about how I felt and what my needs were because it was ingrained in me to be that way, and I didn't know how to heal and evolve from it. I felt as if I couldn't leave him because I needed him to make me feel better. Reflecting back on that makes me feel sad because I really did have options if I wanted to leave. I had family and friends who would have taken me in, so I was in a much better position than some people who didn't have anyone to go to and remained in toxic situations. My self-resentment and trauma convinced me I had nobody to go to and I wasn't worth anything to anyone. So, I stayed and allowed him to cause me pain, slowly killing my self-esteem in the process.

I left Callum at the beginning of April, and by May, I had all new things in my life. During the three years with him, I had tried and failed at being healthier, getting grades for university, passing my driving test, having nice clothes, and going out with my friends because the constant anxiety I had prevented me from being at my best. It's almost like as soon as I closed the door on my life with him, another door flung wide open and all of these gifts fell out and landed right at my feet. All of these treasures had probably been stacked up behind that door, just waiting for me to open it and receive them, but I was never going to have those things because they were not available on my journey with Callum. They couldn't be because I was living a very low vibrational life with him, where the gifts wouldn't have been able to come in, and they certainly couldn't have remained.

Another significant dream that stuck in my mind occurred in the weeks after I had escaped that life with Callum. I was driving behind a lorry, and I looked down to pick up my glasses. When I looked back up, I drove into the back of the lorry, and everything went dark. I stood in complete darkness, but I felt as if I was surrounded by angels, and I felt so peaceful. I asked them, 'Where do I go now?' and a small white light appeared in the distance. I floated towards it. It was at that point that I awoke from the dream, feeling so sure that it was the beginning of my new chapter.

CHAPTER 7

Reclaiming Myself

After a fun summer in 2008, my first in a long time, I joined college in September. It was only a 25-minute drive from home, but I had to have a practice run in the car before I started as I was a very nervous driver. I still couldn't believe that someone like me had been given a licence to drive! I mean, me? Really? I wasn't good enough to do that! I was supposed to do a motorway driving lesson that made me anxious as hell to the point where I kept waking up in the night, stressing over it. Luckily (for me), my driving instructor slipped in his bathroom, cracked his head on the sink and knocked himself out, so I didn't have to go!! Bless him; he was absolutely fine, but I didn't re-book as I couldn't face feeling that fear again.

I made a decision to restrict my world to pacify my fear, and I allowed it to dictate how much of my life I was able to enjoy. I settled to build my life within a 20-mile radius of my home. This was still larger than what I had when I was with Callum, so I accepted those 20 miles as good enough.

I finally bit the bullet and applied for a bachelor's degree in forensic science. I'd wanted to do that for years, but my dad told me I couldn't do it because I was 'shit at maths'. He told me I wouldn't be accepted. I believed him for many years because I'd been conditioned to believe that he knew best, and I wasn't good enough to know what was right for me or what I was capable of. I didn't know myself back then, and I believed that I was shit at everything and that I didn't deserve success. This made it very easy to take his advice and believe everything he said. Vulnerable, powerless people are very easy to control, and I can see how easily a person could become a victim of it.

After leaving Callum and seeing that I was good enough to pass my driving test (another thing people previously told me I wouldn't be able to do) and get into college, I thought I would at least try to apply for the forensics course. I was so shocked when they accepted me! Me? Really?! Surely it was an admin error! I thought they had to be desperate for students, and that was how I got my place. I did feel good, though, because I had done so poorly at my GCSEs, and now, I was being accepted into university! With that, all of those comments came flooding in: 'You're gonna be in debt for the rest of your life.' 'You're never gonna pay off that student loan.' Then, the anxiety started to creep back in. Would I be in £20,000+ debt before I even graduated? It felt scary, akin to putting a noose around my neck. My mum was supportive, though, so I held onto her encouragement to nudge me forward. My uncle was also great, and he moved me into my new accommodation in Bristol.

Once college was over in 2009, it was time to go to university. I looked at the girls I'd hung around with in secondary school up until then and thought, 'They hadn't changed anything in their lives in all that time, so how come my life was changing so rapidly?' It made me feel as if there was something wrong with me because I was different from everyone else around me. I remember thinking, 'Why can't I just be happy staying here?'

I began to punish myself for wanting more out of life. I hated myself for feeling the need to be different and pursuing different goals. I felt safe remaining where I was, even though it was not fulfilling or exciting. The idea of going to university made me feel inferior and like an imposter because I thought only smart, well-travelled, well-spoken people went to uni, and I was none of those things.

I sold my car because I was too scared to drive it from Somerset to Bristol as that far exceeded my 20-mile radius! My anxiety wouldn't allow me to drive there, so I'd applied for accommodation in Bristol, costing me so much more than it would have cost to remain at Mum's and commute in every day. It was only a 40-minute drive, after all.

I moved into a house-share with two Caribbean girls and an Asian girl. I loved living with them. I was exposed to different cultures, beliefs and some great food! I especially loved the Jamaican rum cake one of the girls' mums gave us every time she visited. These girls were a wonderful breath of fresh air, as they were so different from the friends I knew back home. They were way more mature, smart, reliable and independent. I didn't get ditched for the dick by those girls, and they also didn't depend on me for everything; they could take care of themselves. I'd spent so many years carrying Callum and my friends my back ached, and those new girls relieved me of that burden. I learnt a lot from living with those girls, and the whole experience with them and being at uni pulled some confidence out of me.

I don't believe uni is for everyone, and I don't believe you must get a degree in order to have a successful career. However, I do believe that college and university were meant to happen for me because the opportunities came so easily and quickly once I was in a healthier emotional state to reach for them. I believe that if something is meant for you, doors will fly open, and everything will happen quickly and effortlessly. If I had recognised that back then, I would have shared that insight with my friends from those days and encouraged them to expand their lives and follow their goals. However, it was their journey and their choice. Nobody offered me that valuable information; I simply followed my feelings.

Right up until meeting my new housemates and friends in my course, I'd always thought there was something wrong with me. I just felt so different from my friends, with different beliefs, values and priorities. It was only when I went to uni that I started to discover what real friendships were about. Everything just felt so much more authentic with that new group of people, and I felt more connected to them because we shared similar values. Before meeting those new friends, I used to tell people that I preferred hanging around with boys 'cos girls were bitchy. You would NEVER catch me saying that now! Usually, when girls say that, it is because they themselves are bitchy, and therefore, they experience it being given back to them by other girls. Hands up—that was once me. I was incredibly bitchy. You would never see me welcoming a new girl or complimenting anyone. My self-esteem was dangerously low. I couldn't see anything nice in myself, so I certainly didn't have the capacity to see anything nice in anyone else! There was also a lot of anger in me during those times, which restricted my ability to say anything nice to anyone.

My new friends in Bristol introduced me to new ways of dressing and made me feel more comfortable in my skin. I had spent my life hiding my body, desexualising myself as a way to feel safe from the abuse, and it had become an unconscious habit I had yet to break free from. Internally, I felt as if I was growing, so I felt guided to show that growth externally. It did, however, come with its challenges. I still felt ugly, round-shouldered and disgustingly skinny. There was absolutely nothing attractive about me. This perceived self-image influenced my toxic behaviour when it came to men and dating because I felt hideous, so when I was out and a guy would try it on with me, I instantly went for it, even if they were not attractive. Getting with a guy always gave me the validation I could never give myself. The encounters were always short-lived because they were conditional and superficial. It became standard practice to go clubbing and wait to be picked out by one of the guys who spent the entire night standing against the wall of the club, who was seeking the most vulnerable prey for him to catch. I didn't mean anything. I was just pissed and easy to grab hold of as I stumbled past them.

I was anxiously attached to other people's approval and validation because I didn't feel worthy enough to feel it for myself, so I allowed that behaviour to continue and be used. I had come from three years of scraping the bottom of the barrel with Callum, so those subsequent brief encounters held some good moments for me and gave me more life lessons.

CHAPTER 8

Nasty Dex, Nice Dex

During my partying time in Bristol, I met two guys on two separate occasions who didn't know each other, and they were both called Dexter. I labelled them 'Nasty Dex' and 'Nice Dex'. Nice Dex was originally from Barbados whilst Nasty Dex was Nigerian. Nice lived in London whilst Nasty lived in Bristol. Nice Dex earned his title because he spoke nicely to me whilst Nasty Dex shouted at me if I told him 'no,' or I wouldn't do what he wanted. Both of these guys had grabbed me whilst standing on the sidelines of a club dance floor (the usual MO I was accustomed to at that point).

I met Nasty first, and he texted and called me all the time, giving me the validation and approval I required. I was so nervous on our first date because he wanted to meet during the day, and I was self-conscious about meeting in daylight because of how I looked.

My friend did my hair and makeup because I didn't have a clue what to do. I was also nervous because I thought he was way out of my league, and I was definitely punching here. We went to a pub for a drink and chatted away. I don't remember what I said, but about ten minutes into our 'date', I said something he disagreed with, and he immediately wrapped both of his hands around my neck! He didn't squeeze hard, but they were firmly placed there, and he glared at me wide-eyed. I confidently told him, 'Get your hands off my neck,' pointing my finger in his face. Asshole didn't know who he was messing with. I wasn't scared of him in the slightest. He let go of my neck, and we sipped our drinks quietly and resumed talking again as if nothing had happened.

Mistake Number One! That was an enormous red flag that had, quite literally, been wrapped around my neck, and my low self-esteem chose to ignore it, focusing on the fact that I wasn't scared of him and could probably beat him in a fight if it came to it. That is just insane thinking, but it was my way of thinking (and justifying) back then.

He didn't apologise to me; he didn't offer an explanation as to why he had done it, and I betrayed myself by allowing it to go unchecked, encouraging more of that behaviour. I had demonstrated to him how he could treat me, yet I naively expected him to become a transformed character in the following weeks. I was gaslighting myself, which, in turn, allowed him to gaslight me. I became upset when he was nasty and disrespected me, but then I allowed him to do it. At the time, I didn't realise that our first date was him showing me who he truly was, and I showed him that I was not going to call him out on it, enabling him to continue being who he really was. The fact that I tried to change him into who I wanted him to be was insane and only caused me stress and pain. It was like trying to fit a square peg in a round hole: it was not going to work. Only he was capable of changing himself, and I needed to take responsibility for myself. It is all great advice now, but I didn't know it at the time, so I continued on the path to more toxicity. I also blamed him for why I was being treated so poorly and had a victim-like mentality about it. He was, however, responsible for his actions and behaviour towards me. I could have, and definitely should have, cut him loose the moment he strangled me in the pub.

He knew I was easy to exploit, and he said the right things if it fitted in with his narrative at the time (when he wanted sex, basically). Other times, he was just mean. Although it makes me sick to think about how I was back then, the one thing I can be proud of is that everything I did to or for him came from a genuine place. I was kind and respectful to him, and I forgave his poor behaviour, allowing him the freedom to be who he wanted to be, and I didn't criticise or shout at him.

On the other hand, he just was not a nice person. He took advantage of my kindness towards him. He was exploitative, nasty, disrespectful and aggressive, but just because I allowed that behaviour didn't mean he should continue with it. That was a testament to his character, and all that time, I believed there was something bad inside of me. Once again, I was listening to other people's opinions and views on me and ignoring who I really was on a soul level.

During that time, when Nasty dipped in and out of contacting me (only to ask for sex, never to check in to see how I actually was), I met Nice Dex. The manner in which he talked to me, his relaxed body language, and his mature attitude were so refreshing compared to Nasty Dex. He was much calmer in his approach to me, and we spent the next few months talking on the phone as he lived in London, and I was in Bristol. Although he spoke nicer to me than Nasty did, we were not entirely out of the woods. If I missed his call or didn't reply to a text within a couple of hours, he accused me of not being interested in him. I didn't read the signs then, but this was his insecurity projected onto me. He desperately sought attention, and I gave it to him. I wasn't special in his eyes; I was merely there to stroke his ego and fill a void in him, and I allowed him to be there to fill a void in me with respect to validation and approval. I now realise that Nice Dex also had low self-esteem otherwise he wouldn't have been searching that much for attention. If he genuinely wanted to make a connection with me, he would have made more effort to see me. I was essentially a pen-pal for months, but I accepted it because it was a nice respite from Nasty Dex, and I felt much safer being a pen-pal with Nice Dex than being a verbal punchbag with Nasty.

It's crazy how I could have two guys who were polar opposites on the surface, and yet, deep down, they were both just as damaged as I was. Neither of them was emotionally intelligent enough to be nice or respectful. Quite frankly, I had no emotional intelligence either, as I believed their attention was acceptable because, at the end of the day, it was attention.

If I wasn't getting it from someone, I was worthless. If I was getting it, I was worthy.

With this mindset, I was always going to fail.

Nowadays, I would never put up with that behaviour because I like, love and respect myself enough to put a stop to it, and I am comfortable being alone. Being alone does not mean being lonely, and that is something more people need to realise. Release yourself from the stigma of being alone—it is not a negative word!

If I'm not receiving attention now, it doesn't change how I feel about myself at all. I still love and accept myself for who I am, and there is so much power in that feeling. It's actually hard reflecting back on these memories and remembering how I allowed myself to live like that. It's easy to blame other people for the wrongs they did me, and I spent years doing so. However, true healing and growth come when you accept responsibility for your part and learn from it. Power comes from taking ownership and evolving. When you consistently blame others, you become powerless and easier to control by external influences.

If something is not working, makes you feel shit, and you have to change yourself to make that other person like you more, end it. It's not going to get better. Behavioural patterns are deeply ingrained, and unless someone is doing the inner work, they will not change that quickly, particularly if you are changing yourself in order to satisfy their needs.

Take my situation with Callum, for example. I only left because I was close to committing suicide. After being that low, I was definitely not going back to that life. However, as that was an extremely low bar to be at, even a slight improvement left me still scraping the bottom of the barrel. To have not wanting to commit suicide as the reason for ending a relationship is really sad and actually disturbing. Nowadays, I would base it on not sharing the same values or not being emotionally fulfilled, but that's only because I've done the inner work and faced my demons. You don't grow and evolve just by thinking better thoughts; absolutely not. You have to take the time to reflect, take responsibility and weed out the behavioural patterns that keep you stuck attracting the same people, situations and experiences. Reading a few self-help books alone will not make you a reformed character; you have to do the shadow work and face all the shit you have buried inside, take ownership and stop blaming others for how they have treated you. This just attracts more of the same, as this is where your primary focus is.

I spent a long time being angry at the Dexes and blaming them for how our time was spent, but I don't anymore. I have forgiven them because now, I'm aware of behavioural patterns and trauma bonds, and now, I know that we attract into our lives what we put out. I attracted them into my life because, subconsciously, I operated at the same level as them. I hope they have grown because I can honestly say the way all three of us acted and allowed pain into our lives was incredibly exhausting and a huge waste of everybody's time.

The last time I had contact with them was in 2011. Nasty was kicking off at me, yet again, and I told him not to contact me anymore. Within minutes of that conversation, his friend texted me, saying that Dex had given him my number and 'Mans just wanna link you innit.'

I didn't reply.

Nice eventually told me he was coming to Bristol and he would take me out on a date. Once he arrived at mine, he said he just wanted to 'chill' at my house after I had gotten dressed to go out for a meal. He spent the entire evening trying to have sex with me. I kept saying no and pushing him off of me. Once he got the message that I wasn't going to sleep with him, he said he was going to meet a friend in town, and he left, never to be heard from again. It was a pretty long journey to make from London to behave like that, so more the fool he is for being so dumb and thinking that was a good idea.

My experience with the two Dexes should have been enough for me to learn my lesson, spot the signs and not get involved in a similar situation, but as I was not working on myself and taking the time to heal, I remained in my dominant state of low self-worth and fell unconsciously back into that cesspit. It was in that cesspit that I found Hans.

CHAPTER 9

New Adventures Down Under

University gave me so much more than a degree; it gave me the confidence to get out in the world. It was at uni, surrounded by influential and inspiring people, that I realised I had a passion for travelling. Uni really opened my eyes to the world, especially after coming from three blind years with Callum.

I had been on family holidays abroad but had never backpacked or travelled on my own or with people I didn't know. In 2010, my friend introduced me to a man who'd backpacked all over the world, and he made his money taking people on trips with him. I made contact and joined him and a group of strangers to backpack around Eastern Europe. I was so nervous to go, but the support from my friends at uni really encouraged me to go for it. When I told people from back home of my plans, the common comment was, 'Have you seen *Hostel*?' I had seen the film, but that didn't mean it would happen to me, though I must admit the response did make me anxious about the trip. Thankfully, I listened to my gut and went ahead, anyway.

I've since come to realise that people always mock or criticise things they don't understand. The people who made these comments did so with good intentions as a way to ensure I would be safe, I'm sure. However, it's more important to trust your own intuition over others' perceptions. I chose to follow my inner guidance, and I'm so grateful I did because I had such an incredible experience.

Backpacking around Eastern Europe was so rewarding. I was put in a situation where I didn't know anyone, and we had to spend every minute of every day together. I had to adapt quickly because I was spending 24/7 with a group of strangers, with different characters, spending hours packed into a small van, driving through countries and putting up with uncomfortable—and sometimes cold—sleeping arrangements. I was dying for a hotel and a bed instead of a tent or a hostel. Sleeping in the woods of Slovenia and Serbia was the worst because it was raining heavily and freezing. Although I didn't feel safe sleeping in a hostel in Bosnia, at least it was warm.

The entire trip was like nothing I had ever experienced before and something I never thought I would ever be able to do. Getting out of my comfort zone (especially that twenty-mile radius I used to impose upon myself) was incredibly beneficial and character building. I returned to the UK with a wide-open mindset and an eagerness to experience more of the world.

My next trip was to Cape Town, South Africa, volunteering to teach English for GVI, a charity. It was such a fulfilling experience and one I would have continued for a long period of time if I could afford it. South Africa was beautiful, and it was amazing to see all the wildlife. I saw whales in the ocean every morning when we were driving to the school. It was a lovely change from the cars, buildings and grey clouds I saw on my commute to uni most mornings. During my time there, I went shark cage diving. A couple of years ago, I wasn't able to drive away from my hometown, and now, I was face-to-face with seven great white sharks! My life had significantly transformed since I'd decided to believe in myself a bit more and make stuff happen for me rather than expect life to deliver everything to my doorstep.

It is true that you become who you surround yourself with. Since making new friends at uni, I had become more outgoing and adventurous. Those people influenced and motivated me to become the person I never thought I could be. My sense of adventure had been discovered, and I was now in a place, emotionally and mentally, to be able to nourish that. Between 2009 and 2023, I had been to 46 countries, and I know that wouldn't have happened if I had listened to other people's opinions and so-called advice on how I should live my life and what they perceived I was capable of. Abraham Hicks talks about allowing your feelings and emotions to be your compass, so that was what I did when it came to my decision to travel after graduating from university.

A common theme I hear from people is that they would like to go. The best piece of advice I could give is to just do it. There will always be an excuse as to why you can't go. There will always be the anxiety and fear of going. People assume I'm brave for doing a lot of travelling by myself, but that's not the case. I get nervous and apprehensive, but I do it anyway. It's about feeling the fear and pushing on through regardless.

For most of my life, I've felt trapped within my own body, not feeling safe, not feeling at peace, and this manifested in my external life by putting me in situations where I was restricted and unfulfilled. As I began to release myself from my mental prison, my external world opened up on a global scale—literally. The more I chose to do what I was being internally nudged to do, the more confident I got at doing it and the more freedom that came with it. I have a wealth of memories from my travel experiences around the world and a deep sense of contentment from it. It was the most enriching and rewarding experience of my life, and it really did make me grow as a person and realise how capable and independent I really am.

Part of my travelling involved being in Australia for two years. I went over in 2012 with my friend, Rachel. My intention was to stay for three months and move on—Rachel wanted to find sponsorship and live there. This experience was like no other, and it was definitely character building, completely transforming me.

There is something satisfying about being able to go to a new city or country and make a life for yourself. Being somewhere people didn't know me was a great opportunity just to be me without the opinions and warped perceptions of those claiming to know me. The first few months in the country, I wouldn't sit on the beach in a bikini because I hated my body and felt the same deep sense of shame I had had since I was five years old. This soon changed because I was surrounded by the new friends I'd made in the hostel, and they always complimented me for my long legs, my flat stomach and my tall, slender frame. Hearing those words on a daily basis began to dilute the shame I felt around my body, and I started wearing bikinis on the beach, swapped my maxi dresses for shorts and crop tops, and I even stood up straighter. It felt easier to pull my shoulders back and raise my head up, and I felt safer to be seen. This time period made me realise just how powerful words are. When I was told I was ugly, I believed it. Now, I was being told I was 'beautiful' and 'hot', so I began to embody that by standing up straighter and wearing clothes that accentuated my body rather than hiding it.

There's an immense amount of power in being so connected to your inner self that people's negative words cannot damage or affect how you feel about yourself. Their aspersions can't permeate the aura you have developed around you. However, this level of self-acceptance does not come overnight, and you need to do a lot of soul-searching to identify and remove old behavioural patterns and trauma bonds. I naïvely thought that now that I had accepted and liked my body everything would be great, and I was a brand-new person who made better choices. There was some truth to this; however, I still hadn't addressed the demons I'd harboured since I was five, and therefore, my pattern of getting into toxic relationships continued to repeat itself. I was also still at a level where my self-esteem might plummet, and I was extremely self-critical and punished myself for being who I was. That self-hatred had not disappeared because I hadn't taken steps to heal properly. I had only focused on the external by accepting the way I looked. My deep-rooted abandonment and self-worth issues were still there.

Even when I felt better about the way I looked, I still referred to myself as 'horrible' and 'disgusting'. As I told myself this, essentially disrespecting and disliking myself, I manifested people into my life that mirrored how I treated myself. In 2013, one of those people was Hans.

Hans was a German boy who stayed in the same hostel as me. He was a beautiful-looking guy with blonde hair, blue eyes and broad shoulders. The moment I met him, he made me laugh. He asked where I was from, and I said England. He then asked if my English had improved since I'd been in Australia, and I said, 'No, I'm from England,' to which he said, 'Yeah, I know. It was a joke.'

I felt like an idiot, but also found it funny.

Hans asked if he could buy me a drink, and everything started from there. I was still relatively new in Perth, and at the time, I didn't feel secure because I didn't have a job and money was very low, so when Hans came along, he gave me that sense of security and safety I couldn't give myself. One night I was really down because I was applying for jobs and getting nowhere. Hans was really supportive. He put his arm around me and said he would help me out and I would be okay.

That was my first mistake. I looked to him as a form of security and relied upon him to make me feel better. At the time, I didn't know that wasn't sustainable and would only end in pain: mine. It's not someone else's responsibility to make you feel better, and it's dangerous to rely on someone to look after you. In the wrong person's hands, this can lead to abuse financially, physically, mentally and emotionally. You are essentially putting your life into someone else's hands, and they may drop you if you get too heavy to carry or they decide they no longer want to help you. It puts you in a position of powerlessness. Obviously, there will be scenarios where you do rely on help from others, and that's okay, but it's important that you don't put that person in a position where you believe you will lose out if they take away their support.

A few days after Hans said he'd support me, Rachel and I were offered a job in a pub six hours away from Perth. It was only for three months, $20 an hour, food and accommodation included, so we had to accept it. When I told Hans about it, he showed me a different side of his personality: he was cold, rude and dismissive. I also witnessed how horrible he really was because he started saying things in front of me that he hadn't said before. He made references to Hitler being a hero and an inspiration, and he talked about 'blue babies', which meant stillborns, and I couldn't be around him anymore because I found him repulsive. Then, one night at 2.00 a.m., he came into my room, got into my bed and asked for sex. He kept pushing and pushing, ignoring me when I kept saying no.

Eventually, he got the message and turned his back to me to go to sleep. In the morning, he got up and left without acknowledging me. This was the guy I believed was going to be my source of support and security before I found myself a job and my own security. He was only nice to me when he thought I needed him, and he was now showing me that anything between us was purely conditional. The next few days consisted of his ignoring me when he was with his mates and following me to my room, trying to have sex with me, then questioning why I was so difficult when I told him no. I began to think I deserved to be treated like that, and it was my fault he behaved like that. He'd said he would support me and help me, and then I went and got a job away from Perth, so it was my fault he was treating me that way. I punished myself and blamed myself again, simultaneously adopting a victim-like attitude about how I was being treated. I allowed it to make me upset. I focused on it constantly and complained about him to anyone who would listen. The one thing I didn't do was tell him firmly and confidently that I didn't deserve it and I wouldn't accept his behaviour towards me anymore. I didn't allow myself to focus on the better things I had going on in my life, like my new job, a new adventure, increased finances and my new friends. Everything Hans did took my attention and energy, and this, in turn, gave me more of the same.

YOU ARE WHAT YOU FOCUS YOUR ENERGY ON!

When Hans was nice to me, I felt approved of and happy; when he was not nice to me, I felt worthless and a shit person who didn't deserve nice things. He literally had all the power to change how I felt, and subsequently, how my day would pan out. I wasn't evolved enough to feel secure and good enough regardless of his behaviour towards me. His mood controlled my emotions and self-esteem, and I believed I could only feel happiness if he gave it to me.

I have realised that being nice to someone does not necessarily mean they will be nice to you. We get told to treat people how we would like to be treated, and I believed that to be true. Surely, karma would play out, so if I treated someone nicely, they would give it back to me.

How wrong was I?

It was bullshit. The number of guys I had been loyal and faithful to and who had shat on me from a great height demonstrated that treating them how I wanted to be treated meant nothing. With some of those guys, the more I treated them nicely, the more they took advantage. Nowadays, I start treating someone how I want to be treated, but if they don't reciprocate it, I'm out. Fuck it. I'm not hanging around, waiting for them to change and mirror my actions. If they are genuinely decent human beings, they'll treat me well and not take advantage of me. I don't need to hang on in the hope they'll notice I'm doing nice things and then reciprocate.

Once you focus the attention from within and treat yourself the way you would like others to treat you, this begins to sink in subconsciously. Once it becomes your core belief, you naturally attract people into your life who mirror this back to you. Anybody who is truly at peace within does not want to treat people poorly—they just won't be capable of it. Anybody who is at peace will have a much stronger, healthier radar that will immediately identify red flags and take the most appropriate course of action. Some people are just not emotionally intelligent or evolved enough to realise how they hurt other people. That's okay, though; it's not for us to judge them. Everyone is on their own journey and will (hopefully) find their own way to heal and grow. In the meantime, it is not up to anyone else to accept their poor behaviour. They should just be left alone, giving them the opportunity to take responsibility for their own lives.

All of this is great advice, but I didn't know it at the time and continued to allow Hans into my life, hoping he would change to become a better person and make me feel better about myself. On reflection, I had abandoned myself and kept him in my life on the condition that he made me feel better about myself. Therefore, I had manifested a person who would abandon me and keep me in his life on the condition I made him feel better, which, for him, meant sex.

Although this was a very short period in my life, it had an impact on my issues of self-worth and triggered resentment of myself. I didn't realise that someone with that level of hatred for other people would not be nice to me just because I wanted him to be nice. There were years of damage inside that boy, enabling him to be so nasty. Of course, my presence would not resolve that. He was incapable of being nice, but I perceived it as being that I wasn't good enough for him to be nice to me.

This belief carried over into my next situation (or repeated behavioural pattern): Luca.

CHAPTER 10

Bienvenue á Emotional Abuse

Hating the new job, Rachel and I moved back to Perth, to our old hostel, and found jobs in the city. Hans was thankfully gone, but a lot of our friends were still there. Everything felt exciting again—another new adventure! I had a job waitressing in a hotel full-time and was making a lot of money. One Thursday night, I returned to the hostel after work around midnight, and everyone was pissed up on goon (boxed wine). That was the great thing about my hostel: there was always a party going on, no matter the day or the time. I tried three times to get into my room and was accosted by someone each time to have a drink with them, but I was so tired, and my back and feet hurt from waitressing all day and the 40-minute walk home. On my final attempt to get to my room, Luca appeared from behind a door, shouted, 'Hola, Michaela,' then bear-hugged me and asked me for a kiss. It was his second time trying it on with me since he'd moved to the hostel a couple of weeks previously.

The only reason I initially turned him down was because the guy was so ridiculously hot, and I couldn't believe his advances towards me were genuine. All the girls in the hostel fancied Luca, and I didn't believe he would choose me. He was a tall, tattooed French-Italian guy with piercing blue eyes and thick, jet-black hair. He was so handsome, and everyone (including himself) knew it. I believed he was only trying it on because he was drunk, and I refused to believe that he was attracted to me. As I (reluctantly) told him no, his friend, Jerome, came over and said, 'Kayla, he likes you,' so I thought, *Fuck it*, and kissed him. He then asked if he could stay in my room with me, and I let him.

This continued for the next few days. I'd come back from work late, he'd be pissed and come to bed with me. Although I still thought he was way out of my league, I started to feel as if he must have liked me because he was going to bed with me every night despite the fact that he could go to bed with literally any other girl in the hostel. This realisation made me want to have sex with him.

Our first night was spent in the girls' bathroom, going from the showers to the toilet cubicles. We had so much fun! We were both so buzzing afterwards that we kept giggling on the walk back to my room (which I shared with seven other people in bunk beds).

Luca's English was very broken, so we did not communicate well. All we had was a strong attraction and great sex, which was good but not sustainable. Although I was satisfied physically, I was massively unfulfilled emotionally and mentally. Apart from the sex, things were very boring between us, but I ignored it as I thought I was lucky to have him because he was so hot, and I didn't get hot men. I became anxiously attached to him, seeking his validation and approval, believing my self-worth and value were dependent on his opinion of me. I was terrified of losing him because my happiness depended on him; I really hadn't learnt my lesson from previous experiences.

As time went on, I started to get girls asking me if Luca and I were together, what the situation was between us, or if we were serious about each other. My gut instinct told me they were asking for clarification so they knew if they could have something with him, but I refused to listen and convinced myself that they were asking innocently and there was nothing to worry about.

My friends began telling me that when I was at work, Luca flirted with some of the girls. I also noticed that when I walked into a room, any girls near him quickly disappeared once they saw me. If there was nothing untoward happening, then there was no need to leave, right? And this didn't just happen once or twice; it happened a lot. I never asked him why it kept happening as I didn't want him to think I was jealous and controlling because then I would lose him. Again, I suppressed myself and allowed him to continue unchecked. I also allowed myself to continue unchecked, and in turn, more of the same kept happening. I didn't like being vulnerable and talking about my emotions back then. I took it as a sign of weakness instead of the strength that it actually was. I was still of the assumption that you should treat people how you want to be treated, so I lived in the hope that he would recognise how loyal I was to him and reciprocate. Of course, it didn't work; it only gave him the green light to continue doing what he was doing.

I didn't respect or honour myself enough to have an open conversation with him about how I felt and what my boundaries were. Quite frankly, I didn't have any boundaries! If I didn't know what my boundaries were, then he certainly wouldn't know either, but that was still no excuse to treat someone disrespectfully, and if anything, it was a testament to his character for taking advantage of my lack of boundaries.

One night, a boy who was new to the hostel told me that Luca was in the park that day, flirting with this girl (one of the girls who conveniently moved away from Luca when she saw me approaching). He remarked, 'Well, the way he was acting today, I wouldn't have guessed he was seeing someone.'

I'd had enough, so I confronted Luca over it. Of course, he denied it and said the boy was jealous, then went to confront him.

The boy had the nerve to say he never said anything to me! What?

Now, I was even more annoyed! I had finally been given intel I could work with that resonated with my suspicions, and now he denied having said anything to me. So now, I had one guy who was deceiving me behind my back and another who was deceiving me to my face in front of a group of people. Who could I trust, exactly? It was such a common theme in my life, being betrayed by people all the time. I just expected it now, and nothing seemed to surprise me anymore. I accepted that nobody had my back, and that was the hand life had dealt me.

Luca went to hit the boy, but I pulled him back in time. Then, we went to my room, out of the way. Luca assured me the boy was causing trouble, so I shouldn't listen to him. I chose to believe Luca because the boy had clearly demonstrated he couldn't be trusted either, so I was back to square one, except this time, Luca knew he could get away with more than he already had because I had allowed it to be swept under the carpet, with very little explanation and without telling him how it made me feel. It was a big mistake because it was my opportunity to tell him that I wasn't happy being with him, and I didn't feel as if he was treating me in the way I deserved to be treated. My anxious attachment and misinformed belief that his approval was evidence of my worth suppressed my true feelings and set me up for the road ahead.

Things only got worse from that point. He knew he had me, and in true narcissistic style, he took advantage of it and played on my insecurities to justify his behaviour and his treatment of me.

He started criticising the way I dressed. He hated me wearing skirts, dresses or low-cut tops. I was an English girl in Australia—I was boiling! Perth averaged 35C, and he tried to get me to cover up. He was insane. One way to prevent me from wearing low-cut tops was to bite my chest and thighs during sex, leaving bite marks and bruises on me so I would have to cover them up. Sex between us was rough anyway, so I thought the biting was a part of it until, one day, a boy who was sharing my 8-bed dorm in the hostel, walked into my room while I was getting changed and asked why I had the marks on me. I told him that Luca had done it, and Luca immediately admitted that it was to keep me covered up. I feel, in his own weird way, his admission to the boy was a way of showing off how much power he had over me, but that soon stopped when the boy told him it was disgusting and not to do it to me again. Luca then got in a strop, stormed out of the room and sulked all day, not speaking to me until the next morning. From then on, I knew his game and started wearing low-cut tops and shorts, freely explaining to anyone who asked why I had bite marks over my body. Exposing him put a stop to his biting.

Luca did, however, continue to tell me what to wear, especially if I was going for a night out. I always wanted to go on nights out with Luca, either with his friends, mine or as a group, but he never wanted to.

He never wanted to include me in anything. My only job was to work, make money and wait at the hostel to give him sex after he had been out with his friends, bearing in mind that he was with them all the time because none of them worked. They were the laziest bastards I have ever known, and this is coming from someone who used to be with a jobless addict, but at least he tried to work before the drugs had taken over. Luca and his mates had no addiction that prevented them from working; they just didn't want to. They wanted to sell drugs instead and shoplift. Luca spent his days bumming around the hostel, doing anything that didn't involve spending money (except buying alcohol) and flirting with other girls while I was out working. Then, he had the nerve to question me about the price of the items I bought from the shop on the way home or tell me I wasn't allowed out or I could go out if I covered up. I just used to tell him to bugger off when he questioned how much money I had spent because, after all, it was MY money, not his. I also refused to change my outfits because he was always out on the piss, and I had to hear stories of him flirting with other girls, so I was not about to pacify him. There ended up being a lot of point-scoring between us, and it wasn't healthy.

I had been presented with so many red flags, and I'd batted each of them out of my way. I was too insecure to leave him, so I settled for point-scoring, which was so exhausting, and it was a game I was never going to win. A person with good intentions never wins against a narcissist, because narcissists are incapable of emotion and taking accountability. It was easy for him to break me down, but he was hard for me to break because he didn't care enough about my feelings.

I adored that guy. I thought I was so lucky to have him because he was way out of my league. I never so much as looked in another man's direction when I knew I had Luca to go to, but he just couldn't see it. He judged me by his own standards, accusing me of going off with another man when I went out, even though he was the one linking up with other women. He once timed how long it took me to walk from the hostel to my friend's house and accused me of meeting up with someone when I arrived there ten minutes later than I should have done. It was because I had taken a detour into a shop, but he was so suspicious and jealous over it that he sulked and wouldn't talk to me for a day. When he withdrew, it triggered my abandonment wounds, and it made me react in a way he didn't deserve, such as anxiously over-explain my behaviour and my movements in the hope that he would come back to me because I didn't believe a girl like me could attract a man as hot as him.

This is another example of how not liking yourself places you in horrible situations with horrible people. I would never put up with his treatment now, and it disappoints me that I let that into my life, believing that he was the answer to my childhood wounds. He really wasn't, and to be honest, he had an accumulation of his own. Hurt people hurt people, and that's what he was doing, hurting me to make himself feel better. He chased other women to make himself feel validated and approved of. He had a dismissive-avoidant attachment style, whereby he used people to fulfil his needs and then dismissed or avoided that person once it got too emotional. That style of person cannot process or regulate their emotions, so they are incapable of processing other people's emotions. Luca struggled with expressing emotion, which manifested as bitterness, jealousy and aggression. He tried to strangle me once and hit me a couple of times, but I hit him back each time, so he soon stopped trying. As if he would get away with that. He might have gotten away with trying to sleep with other women because I had no proof he was actually sleeping with them, but he was not getting away with hitting me. I'd happily fight him all day long, as I had plenty of pent-up anger to fuel me and keep me going.

One night, I went back to the hostel after work, and Luca was pissed, as usual. I got ready to go out with my friend for a late dinner, and Luca tried to put a stop to it. He pulled me into bed and tried to have sex with me and told me not to go out. This went on for bloody ages, and he wouldn't let me go while I kept trying to get ready. When my friend came into my room to get me, Luca threatened to get with another girl if I went out, and I went anyway. On my way out, he purposely grabbed one of his female friends and began kissing her face, but she pushed him away. I knew he was doing it to wind me up, but I ignored it and left the hostel. I trusted that girl and didn't believe she would do anything with him.

I was only out for an hour, but I had this overwhelming sense of anxiety that he was up to something. I really couldn't relax and asked my friend if we could go back. When we got back to the hostel, I headed straight for my room to see if he was in bed; he wasn't. I went to his friend's room; he wasn't there either. My stomach was doing somersaults as I looked over at the bedroom door of the female friend Luca had kissed earlier. I was nervous to go in there, but I took a deep breath and headed over. I flung the door open and switched on the light, just in time to catch her jumping off of him as he lay in her bed. She had been sitting on top of him, with her legs on either side of him. Fair enough—they were both fully clothed, but his jeans were undone, so I probably caught them before they had gone too far. There were three bunk beds in that room—why was he in hers? More to the point, why wasn't he in mine?

I stormed over there. 'What the fuck is going on?'

He didn't say anything.

She put her head in her hands and said, 'It's not what it looks like.'

I hit her across the face and screamed at her to get out (even though it was her room). I was fucking raging! I kept shouting at him to tell me what was going on, but he wouldn't say anything, and it made me angrier. I started hitting him, then I strangled him and dug my nails into his face. The pent-up aggression I'd had for so long just unleashed in that one moment. Then I saw his trainers next to the bed, so I picked them up and began hitting him with them.

My friend pulled me off, and I started to walk out, but then I noticed a plastic chair being used to dry someone's washing. I picked it up and threw it at him; the clothes flew everywhere. Everybody who slept in the room hid themselves under their duvet covers, and I don't blame them—I was ready for anything with anyone at that point.

The girl asked if she could explain to me what had happened, and as Luca was giving me nothing, I accepted the offer. We went to the girls' toilets, and she told me that after I'd left, he was messing around, trying to kiss her, but nothing happened. It was just a joke. Then he followed her to bed, but she didn't know why. Apparently, when I walked in, she was climbing over him to get out to go to the toilet.

I was a whole bag of emotions by that point and didn't know what to believe anymore. All I'd wanted was to have a drink with my friend after a ten-hour shift of waitressing, and he had punished me for it. The girl told me not to trust Luca and advised me not to be with him anymore.

I was bloody fed-up by then and went to my room with my friend to process what the hell had just happened. We saw Luca in the corridor, coming out of the bedroom, his fly still undone and his trainers in his hand. I don't know where he went and didn't care; I was fuming.

The next day, he tried to talk to me, but I was so down and exhausted about everything. Not only was I over what had happened the night before, but I was over everything he had ever done to me. I didn't want to talk to him because I knew he would put on a good talk and convince me how wonderful he was, and how it was my fault, and that I needed him in my life. I already blamed myself for everything, so I didn't need him to tell me the same. I needed space.

All the next day, I had people telling me that Luca and that girl would never do that to me; I was wrong, I should apologise and so on. They literally invalidated my feelings and completely disregarded how Luca had treated me. For a long time, my gut feeling was that he hadn't been treating me well, and that night was a reflection of what he thought of me; I would never have done that to him.

I stayed at my friend's apartment for the next couple of nights, so I didn't have to see him around the hostel. When I returned, my friend told me that Luca had been wandering around the hostel, lost and not knowing what to do with himself. I really didn't care—I had nothing left to give.

Over the next couple of weeks, Luca kept texting me, asking to meet up and talk, but I wasn't ready, so I ignored all of them. It was another opportunity to break my attachment to him and leave him for good, but I didn't take it and ended up getting back with him. I wasn't aware of patterns and lessons at the time, so I believed everything would be different the next time around, but it really wasn't.

It was actually much worse.

CHAPTER 11

The Second Time Around

Life continues to give you the same lessons over and over until you learn from them and break the cycle, and because neither of us had learnt our lesson, we just repeated more of the same, and subsequently, were in much more pain.

I thought that leaving him those couple of weeks would teach him a lesson not to do that again, but it didn't because that's not how it works. You can't teach a person who doesn't want to be taught. We are also not responsible for other people's actions and must only focus on our own. What I should have done was to ask myself what I was doing that kept attracting those same situations into my life and what I could do to ensure it didn't happen again.

I love this quote from the Civil Rights Campaigner, Rita Mae Brown:

'The definition of insanity is doing the same thing over and over again and expecting different results.'

I'd heard it hundreds of times over the years, but it never clicked in my head until I was 36! A whole ten years after Luca and I had been together. I just wasn't evolved enough to resonate with this before.

In June 2013, myself, Rachel, Angela and Lucie hired a campervan to do a road trip of the West Coast of Australia, all the way to Darwin. On our last night in Perth, Angela asked Luca and his friend, Leo, if they wanted to come along with us, and they both said yes. I was so happy that Luca was coming too. I dreaded leaving him behind because, deep down, I knew he required too much female attention to remain faithful to me, but at the same time, my gut feeling was that I had to put myself first and go on that road trip. If Luca liked me that much, we would meet again.

Yet again, life had given me a doorway out of my 'situationship' with Luca, and I didn't take it. If I were secure enough about myself, I would have recognised that he wasn't going to remain faithful to me, and therefore, he wasn't worth spending any more time on. However, my anxious attachment style jumped at the chance of bringing him along on the road trip and keep him where I could see him.

Of course, we had an awful time together—why would we have a good time? Nothing had changed in either of us as people; it was only our location that had changed.

We girls had planned the road trip out over three weeks so we could spend time in certain places on the way. Of those three weeks, 98% of the time, Luca and I spent it hating each other. He made me cry most days.

I hated him, and I hated myself. He had complete control over my moods. When he was nice to me, I was happy. When he was mean to me, I was upset. He always complained, and nothing was ever good enough. Whatever the group wanted to do, he would want to do the opposite. It was like he was actively seeking out problems because he didn't understand the concept of peace and harmony. I think he felt as if he were in familiar territory when there was conflict, so he made sure he was surrounded by conflict. His unhappiness made me feel as if I wasn't good enough because I couldn't make him happy, and I felt responsible for making him happy, not realising at the time that it would never work. You can't make a person happy if their dominant feelings are unhappiness or discontentment.

Yet again, I was fighting a battle I was never going to win, and it chipped away at me. It was like trying to climb a ladder with no steps—it's not going to happen if the ladder doesn't have the steps in place for you to climb, so you can keep trying, but you will just exhaust yourself and not move from where you are. I would have had a much more enjoyable road trip if I had only realised that Luca was the one responsible for his own happiness, and if he didn't want to try, then that was on him, not me.

Luckily, the girls were great, and the four of us were always talking and laughing with each other. We didn't fall out once. The boys, however, bickered all the time with each other and then stopped talking to each other. Whichever one wasn't sulking would sit with us girls in the evening and have a drink and a laugh while the other one sat alone in the campervan. They seemed to take turns sulking as if it were shift work.

Although Luca was horrible every day, there were a few occasions that stood out the most. One night, I put on some high-waisted jogging bottoms because we were out in the desert, and it was freezing. He didn't wait a second to say, 'What are you wearing? Why don't you wear something sexy for me? All of the girls wear trousers down to here,' and he pointed beneath my hips.

I was instantly overwhelmed with emotion because I already felt inferior to him, and now he was just adding insult to injury. It was a cold night, for fuck's sake! Let me wear warm trousers!

I was so mad and shouted back, 'Why the fuck should I wear something sexy for you when you've been such a dick all day?' The knob had ignored me all day, complaining about money (even though he hadn't paid any money towards hiring out the campervan that we girls had paid for), and all day, I had worn a crop top and a tight-fitting skirt—that was fucking sexy! Not once did he comment on how I looked, but as soon as I put on the jogging bottoms, he was straight in there with a comment. The guy was horrible, and he enjoyed making me feel like shit.

A few days later, I was wearing a tight-fitting dress and a large sunhat. The girls said I looked lovely. Luca looked me up and down and said, 'I don't like your hat.' I cried at that point because I couldn't take any more of his rejection and criticism. This had been going on for months, and his words were eroding my already small self-esteem.

The next evening, we bought some rum because we had been on the road all day, and we sat outside, drinking, all except for Leo, who was sulking in the campervan. The more I drank, the more emotional I got over my situation with Luca and how low I felt.

Angela took me to the toilets so we could have a private chat. Within minutes, Rachel came in, asking if I was okay, as Luca had told her I'd left because I was jealous he was talking to her.

What?!

Where had that come from?!!!!

If he was genuinely concerned that I was jealous, why hadn't he asked me rather than stir up trouble between my friend and me? The betrayal and rejection I felt from him was boiling over, fuelled by the rum, and I lost it. I stormed back to the seating area, but he was gone. Lucie said he was in the van (hiding, no doubt, after throwing a hand grenade into the group).

I found him and shouted at him for talking bullshit as well as for being such an asshole about everything. He didn't look up from his phone and completely ignored me, so I smacked the phone out of his hand. He jumped up and went for me, chasing me through the campsite until I was blocked by some trees. I turned to face him, and he pinned me up against the tree by my neck (it was not the first time he had done this, so I wasn't surprised). I hit him, and he let go and went back to the van. I went back to my friends. This had become a toxic pattern we both contributed to, and it wasn't normal or healthy. Luca and I should not have been together. All we did was hurt each other and ourselves. That's what happens when two broken people get together: they project their self-hatred onto the other person. I used to question why Luca didn't just leave me if he didn't like me—he had plenty of options because he was such a good-looking boy. The fact that he didn't leave me made me think there was something there worth holding onto. I didn't leave him because I didn't believe I would find anything better.

Once we arrived in Darwin, everything changed between us again—new location, new men around us, new Luca! We girls checked into a hostel while Luca and Leo chose to sleep in a tent in a park because they didn't want to pay for a hostel (shocker). Once Luca had seen all the guys in our hostel, he transformed into this wonderful, caring, affectionate character. He became everything I had wanted him to be over the last few months. Being in Darwin was another opportunity life had given me to leave Luca, and again, I chose not to take it up.

We only spent a couple of weeks in Darwin before Lucie went back to Belgium, Angela went to Thailand and Rachel went to Adelaide to do three months of regional work to get her second-year-working holiday visa, which was a requirement of the Australian government.

The two weeks in Darwin was the best time Luca and I ever had with each other, and I thought we had turned a corner. He mentioned that he wanted to go back to England with me when our visas expired, but I wasn't sure if I believed him. Until one day I used his laptop and I saw that he had been online, looking at jobs in England for French-speakers. This blew my mind, and I was over the moon! I enjoyed every moment we had together because I knew I had to leave again soon. I had five months left on my working holiday visa, so I needed to do regional work for three months to get my own second-year visa. The girls had left Darwin, Luca and Leo were still not working or doing anything with their days, and I was fast running out of money. I needed to find a job quickly.

One afternoon, I found a job on a farm back in Western Australia, two hours south of Perth. The farm also contained a dog-boarding kennel business. I was definitely keen to work with dogs, so I called the farmer, and she offered me the job, asking me to start in two days' time. I had to snap it up before someone else took it. I really didn't want to leave Luca now that we were doing so well, but I was in Australia to travel, not to spend my days bumming around in one place with a guy who had no desire to explore the country.

I searched for a flight for the following day and put it on my credit card. Then, I had to do the hardest part: tell Luca.

Arrrrghhhhh—that was such a horrible moment! We were outside the internet café when I told him. He didn't say anything. He just hugged me. Then we walked through town for a bit in silence. He asked if I wanted an ice cream, so I sat on the wall outside of the shop while he went in to get one—it was the only time he had ever bought me anything in the months we had been together, so I knew it was serious.

We sat in silence on the wall, eating our ice creams. At one point, I couldn't hold myself together anymore and started crying. He began crying, too, which made me cry even more because it hurt to see I had made him upset. Leaving him was the hardest thing I had to do, but I knew it was the right decision. Luca suggested paying the farmer off to fraudulently declare that we had both done our three months of regional work, but I wasn't up for that. Getting that second-year visa was important to me, and I wasn't going to risk losing it by paying someone off. I needed to do it properly. That was just Luca's character though. He was not a hard worker, by any means.

I cried on and off for the rest of the day. It was awful. My last night in Darwin, I slept in Luca's tent, that he had set up illegally in a park because he didn't want to pay for a hostel.

My alarm went off at 5.45 a.m. The day had come, and I was scared and sad to leave him. Luca stroked my hair and my face, saying, 'I really like you,' and I really believed that he did.

I was late getting to the coach, and the driver shouted at me to hurry up, so Luca and I didn't have long to say goodbye. On the coach, looking out the window, I saw Luca walk away with his head down, and it literally broke me knowing I had done that to him.

CHAPTER 12

Echoes of Past Errors

Once in Perth, I took a coach to a country town called Brookton and started my job that day. I was working with two other backpackers: an Irish girl and a Canadian girl. They were such lovely people and really did make me feel welcome. We fed and cleaned up after the farm animals and the dogs in the boarding kennels during the day, cooked and ate with the farmers in the evening and watched films together in our caravan before bed. The farmers were actually not that nice, particularly the husband. He was a bullying, racist, homophobic, misogynistic bellend. He was not nice to the animals, his wife or his kids (who were now young adults living across the road).

Luca told me he was going back to perth and he would come visit me in Brookton, as I couldn't leave as the job was seven days a week, and Perth was two hours away. Then, a couple of days later, he told me he was stopping off in Broome before going to Perth to meet his friend, who had driven up from Perth some weeks beforehand. Turns out the friend had been pulled over by the police in Broome, and they found weed, mushrooms and pills in his car, so he was put in prison. He called Luca, asking for $3,000 bail money, and Luca gave him the money. This had me stumped—where had the money come from? That sponger hadn't offered to give us girls any money for the campervan we had paid for, he hadn't contributed to any petrol, and he never paid for any hostel in either Perth or Darwin—where had the $3,000 come from?

Then, I discovered that Luca had bought this boy's car off of him for $2,000. What the fuck? Which orifice had he pulled the $5,000 out of? The only time he'd put his hand in his pocket had been to buy me that one ice cream after I had told him I was leaving Darwin.

When I raised this with him, he responded, 'But it's my friend.'

So, I wasn't your friend, then? Was I not your friend who essentially paid for your travel up the west coast of Australia?

He knew I was broke by the time we got to Darwin, and he chose not to help me out, even though he'd had a free ride up there, all expenses paid for by the girls and myself. I ate one meal a day in Darwin because I needed to save what little money I had left, and he never thought of dipping into his secretive $5,000 to buy some food.

He began gaslighting me, accusing me of not allowing him to help his friend out, which was not the case at all. I was only questioning why he had not used the money to contribute to the trip we had all gone on. He was so stingy, selfish and only interested in his own needs. I would never have had the nerve to sponge off of someone and not pay my way if I had the money to do so.

It was another opportunity to leave him that I ignored.

When he arrived in Perth on the Monday, he called me and seemed really happy to be back in our old hostel. I was happy for him and super-excited to see him when he was coming to visit on the weekend. I spoke to him again on Tuesday, and everything was fine. Then, on Wednesday, everything changed. I didn't hear from him on Wednesday or Thursday, which was weird because we had been speaking every day; something felt off.

I called him on Friday, and he didn't answer, so I tried again later, on a withheld number, and he answered. When he said, 'Hello?' he sounded normal.

As soon as I said, 'All right?' he exhaled deeply and gave a half-arsed, 'Yeah.' He didn't sound as if he wanted to hear from me. I was ultra-paranoid at that point; my heart was pounding, and I started breathing rapidly. I was nervous as hell about what was going on. I heard that he was driving, and then I heard a girl in the background, talking to someone. Nobody answered her, so I assumed she was on the phone.

Luca told me he couldn't talk because he was driving, and he would call me later.

The call ended. I now knew he was in the car with some girl. My paranoia quickly morphed into knowing. He'd definitely met someone else. He'd ghosted me for three days, and now there was a girl with him in his car.

A half-hour later, he called me. I asked if he was still coming to see me tomorrow, and he said, 'I don't think so, 'cos I have met a girl.' His words felt like a kick in my stomach. The adrenaline shot through me, and I felt sick. He went on to say he'd met this girl in a club on Wednesday night. He liked me, but he didn't come to Australia to be in a relationship. He wanted to see me again, but just not tomorrow because it was not fair on that girl, bla… bla… bla… bla… bla.

I couldn't process everything he was saying to me, but it 'wasn't fair' on her? He'd only known her forty-eight hours! Twat! All those times he'd gone on at me, accusing me of getting with other guys when I went out, and he'd done it to me! The audacity of that prick. I was so shocked that had happened.

Knowing what I know now about healing work, it doesn't surprise me that this happened. In fact, it's actually predictable. How we treat ourselves is always mirrored back to us by other people. I had betrayed myself from the moment I'd gotten with Luca. I'd always put his needs before mine, leaving myself feeling like shit in the process. Therefore, I'd manifested someone who also didn't consider my needs and made me feel like shit in the process. I'd betrayed myself to invest in him, and he'd betrayed me to invest in someone else. This was a universal law I wasn't aware of at the time, so I had no idea what I was unconsciously creating in my life. I used to believe that if I'd treated him better, he would have treated me better, but it doesn't work like that.

On our road trip, Lucie had introduced me to this book called *The Secret*. As many people know, this is all about thinking better thoughts, but a lot of it is bullshit. It's not thinking better thoughts that create our lives; it's the feelings and beliefs behind those thoughts that influence what happens in our lives. I'm grateful I read *The Secret* because it opened up my eyes to another world and set me up on a path of discovery. However, to really experience true manifestation, you must understand your emotional guidance and resolve deep-rooted traumas. It's not easy and it's certainly not something you learn from reading one book. In fairness, *The Secret* does advise that your feelings should match your thoughts, but mastering this requires more than reading a book.

That week, the farmers at my workplace were having issues with their son across the road. Basically, the son's father was a bully, and now that his son was an adult, he could fight back. Twice that week, the father and son got into a scrap. The police were called after the father was put in hospital following their second fight. Following this, we girls were told to stay away from the son and his wife (even though we had made friends with them already), and we were not allowed to acknowledge them if they said hello to us from across the road. Like, for fuck's sake; as if this was our problem—you both treat your son like shit.

It was far too dysfunctional for me, given the news I had just had from Luca a few days before. I was in a tiny, secluded country town with just two people for company, working seven days a week, restricted on that farm with those terrible farmers. I had to get away from them and their constant drama. The two backpackers I was with would both complete their three months in a couple of weeks, and I really didn't fancy being alone with the farmers, so I decided to leave. Rachel told me there was a job picking oranges on a farm in Adelaide and a spare room in her share house, so I accepted it. I told the farmers I was leaving and caught the coach to Perth the next day, where I spent the week before flying to Adelaide.

From a mutual friend, Luca found out that I was back in Perth and texted me, asking how I was. I didn't reply—what was there to say? He'd still chosen that girl over me.

Later that day, he texted again, apologising for doing 'bullshit' to me and saying that he missed me. That was when I started believing that my 'positive thoughts' had manifested him back, so I replied to him.

We texted back and forth, and it was really lovely until he asked what I was doing. I told him I was going to the tattooist to buy a new bar for my vagina piercing, and he slipped back into his normal self saying, 'Why? Who do you want to show your pussy to?' Like, really? As if that should be any of his concern now that he was with someone else. The truth was that I just wanted a blue one instead of my green one; it really was that simple.

Then, he started with the manipulation, saying, 'You don't like me anymore, do you? I really like you, and I want to see you again.'

That won me over, so I replied, saying that I'd missed him.

He didn't reply. Of course. I should have known that was his way of making sure I was still invested in him, even though

I was not with him, and he had no intention of getting back with me. He just needed to know that he still had control.

When he didn't reply, I began hating myself for coming across too strong and needy. At the time, I didn't see that the reason he didn't reply was because he was a damaged, insecure, emotionally abusive individual who craved female attention to feel good about himself. Once his needs had been met, he felt superior and in control. I always thought I was the bad one, but despite my insecurities, I never emotionally manipulated him so I could feel in control. That was just cruel.

One night, during my short stay in Perth, I met friends at the old hostel for drinks, and Luca asked one of them if we were going out because I 'looked so hot'. I was just wearing trainers, leggings and a long-sleeved top! Anyway, it shouldn't be his concern when he was still seeing that other girl. When he saw me getting into a guy's car to go into town, he texted, saying, 'Fuck off.' I replied, asking why, and he said, 'Just fuck off.' I ignored it, so he texted again a few hours later, asking where I was and what I was doing. The audacity of that guy. He'd ended it with me for someone else but didn't want to lose control over me. He enjoyed my giving him attention and couldn't stand the thought of me investing my energy elsewhere. It was poisonous, but I'd mistaken it for his genuinely wanting me back. I thought his texts proved he felt something for me, so I contacted him the following day to smooth things over and start afresh.

He replied, saying he didn't want to talk to me because I hadn't spoken to him the night before.

Arrrrggggghhhhhh!

That boy! He was so intent on controlling the situation, and he never considered my feelings, only his own. It was as if he wouldn't allow me to be upset and take some time away to think. If I didn't respond to him on demand, he kept trying and trying until he got me where he wanted me, then turned his back on me. It was his pattern of toxic behaviour that I just wasn't aware of at the time, so I continued, hoping he would become the person I wanted him to be if I kept complying with him.

The reason I couldn't speak to him was because I still felt hurt, betrayed and rejected after he had finished with me for someone else, then ignored me when I told him I missed him after he had reached out to me. If I had my way, we would still be together, and none of that bullshit would have happened in the first place. He was either too thick to recognise this, or too spiteful to care about my feelings and how I was coping.

My abandonment wounds were triggered again, along with all the feelings of not being good enough and hating myself for handling the situation all wrong. I analysed everything I did and what I should have done.

That night, I went to my friend's leaving do at my old hostel and saw Luca there, trying to kiss a girl (that wasn't the girl he was dating at the time). I was not happy—I was upset and jealous. I couldn't even think about kissing another guy, and there he was, trying it on with that girl while he had another girl out there somewhere waiting for him.

My face was absolute thunder and when the girl saw me staring at them, she walked away from him. The girl knew that Luca and I used to see each other, and she knew I wouldn't hesitate to kick off when I got angry.

Luca clocked me and came over to say hi. When I went to the girls' toilets, he followed me into a cubicle. We stayed in that cubicle for just under an hour, kissing and talking. He told me he really liked me, he was sorry for everything and he wanted to come to England with me. I believed him because it felt nicer than the alternative. The truth hurt far too much, so I kept up the delusion to feel at peace. I was so much in denial that I didn't pay attention to the next red flag he presented to me that night: he pinned me up against the wall by my throat, then quickly let me go, laughed, and said, 'I prefer you when you're scared of me.' I wasn't scared of him—it just shocked me as it had come out of nowhere. He looked so proud of himself, with his head held high and chest puffed out.

I just laughed at him and said, 'I ain't scared of you,' and we moved on to a different conversation.

He invited me back to his place, so I went. I didn't care about sleeping with him behind the other girl's back because, as far as I was concerned, he was mine when she had gotten her hands on him. He had also just told me he wanted to come back to England with me, so it felt like what we had ran much deeper than what he had with her.

I stayed the night as his, and it was so comfortable and familiar, like nothing had changed between us.

Two days later, it was my final night in Perth before flying to Adelaide. Luca texted, asking what my plans were, and I told him when I would be at the old hostel to say goodbye to people. When I walked into the hostel, he saw me, put his head down and walked straight out without acknowledging my presence. I assumed he would be back in to say goodbye, but he never returned. His friend Leo came in to give me a hug and wish me good luck in Adelaide. He then apologised and said that Luca wouldn't be coming back in to say goodbye because he had plans.

I couldn't believe it. I was shocked. Why would he have asked what my plans were? What had he intended by asking me that? Why had he not just said goodbye when he walked past me in the hostel? Why did his mate have to apologise on his behalf?

My friend and I just stared at each other in disbelief. It had only been an hour ago that he had texted me. He knew we were coming over, and he'd completely ignored me! So many thoughts and emotions overcame me, the main ones being rejection and feeling unimportant.

When my friend Angela and I got back to our hostel later that night, I fell on the bed and sobbed. Angela must have heard the pain in my sobs as she put her head on my lap as a form of comfort. She didn't say a word. There was nothing to say—how could you explain away what had just happened? It was a very clear, very intentional act of pain he'd inflicted there, and it fucking hurt.

The next morning, I left for Adelaide, and it was such a painful journey. The men sitting in my row of seats on the plane kept talking to me, so it kept my mind off Luca. Once we landed in Adelaide, I rushed to the toilets to cry. I had to hold it in the whole flight, and I just needed a little release. Once composed, I got my bags and took a taxi into town, leaving my bags in storage at the bus station. I had three hours before my coach came to take me to the little country town where I would be staying for the next two months.

I walked around the city, crying. I hid my tears behind my sunglasses but couldn't keep my cries quiet. I just felt so alone, lost, uncertain and anxious. I genuinely had no idea what I was doing or where I was going anymore. I felt completely powerless and as if I had no control over my life. I missed my life at the old hostel with my friends and Luca, of course. Now, I was separated and lost. I also felt as if it was all my fault for choosing to do the regional work over staying in Darwin with Luca. I called myself an idiot for making that decision. I spent the entire three hours crying, walking the streets, sitting on a park bench and even when I was in a café getting lunch. I just couldn't stop. I grieved for many losses: Luca, my friends and myself.

When I collected my bags from storage, the man working there saw that I had been crying and asked if he could do anything to help me. My reply was, 'Not unless you have a time machine.'

It was a three-hour journey to the country town of Waikerie. I spent the first half hour crying quietly, then the next two and a half consumed in a pit of negative thoughts, regret and self-hate. The anxiety in my stomach was overwhelming, and I didn't feel well at all. I just wanted to go back to how things were before we had all left for our road trip to Darwin.

The next two and a half months in Waikerie consisted of picking oranges, packing oranges in a warehouse, pulling onions from fields and cutting stems off garlic from a conveyor belt. They were all physically and mentally demanding jobs, which also gave me plenty of time to think, ultimately causing me more pain. I was so anti-social because of it, and I couldn't hold a conversation with anyone as I wasn't able to get out of my own head long enough to concentrate on what anyone else had to say. I just wanted to be alone in my self-pity and punish myself for the choices I made that had gotten me to that point. I was punishing myself, and in turn, I manifested a life that had punished me, too.

During that time, I was so broke. I had to plan my meals carefully. A grapefruit was enough for two meals—half for breakfast and half for dinner. Lunch generally consisted of pasta or a tin of peas.

Rachel and our new friend Alice tried so hard to get me out socialising and keeping me occupied. I'm glad they did because otherwise, I would have completely withdrawn from everything and ended up in the same mind set I had when I was with Callum.

A week after arriving in Waikerie, Luca texted me saying, 'How are you, crazy girl?' and again, just like that, my mood immediately transformed, and I was happy again. I asked why he had ignored me the other day at the hostel, and he said he didn't know why he did what he did, but he really liked me and wanted to see me again. It felt good to hear, but that feeling quickly disappeared when Angela told me later that day that Luca was still with that other girl. It wasn't what I wanted to hear, and it didn't match up with what he had just said to me. How could he like me and still be with that other girl?? I didn't want to even look at another man, yet he was able to split his energy into two.

From then on, Luca dipped in and out of contact, telling me he missed me, commenting on my photos on social media, saying things like 'Suck my dick,' 'Sexy bitch' and 'Be careful,' for one photo where I was standing next to a boy he didn't know. It was exhausting. He was exhausting. I felt like shit every day. I was either living in the past, feeling grief, or thinking ahead into the future, feeling anxious. I never focused on the present, and because of that, I wasn't healing. I was just prolonging my negative state.

In October, we both agreed we would meet again in January when I was due to go back to Perth. I was happy but also super anxious because I felt as if he wouldn't wait that long. It was frustrating, wishing my time away, not enjoying my present and being eager to get back to him before I lost him again. I put a lot of pressure on myself. My thoughts of us being happily reunited were based on hope. My thoughts of his betraying me again were very real. This is another example of how manifestation works: I attracted that which I felt to be true. My feelings surrounding Luca's finding another girl between October and January were so strong and felt so real that they actually materialised. He did get with a new girl; I discovered it when she began tagging him in photos on Facebook, and those familiar feelings of betrayal came back. I don't know why I believed he would change.

CHAPTER 13
New Zealand, New Problems

After our three months of regional work were completed in December, Rachel and I treated ourselves to a trip to New Zealand. We started off in Christchurch and travelled up the South Island to Nelson and then over to the North Island, stopping to see friends along the way on both islands. Friends we met in Australia had gone to various parts of New Zealand, so we combined seeing them along with exploring the beautiful country.

Once in Wellington, we stayed in a hostel with our friend Clare, a French girl we knew from Perth. Our first night there with Clare was so much fun—we had pizza and spent the evening drinking. I felt so good up until when Clare decided to tell me that Luca had kissed Loo behind my back one night when we had all lived in the old hostel.

What the fuck?

Excuse me?

Loo, the friendly, smiley, innocent-looking Swedish girl?

Oh, wow!

The same old feelings of betrayal came back again. For fuck's sake, give me a break! How much more of this shit did I have to take? Why did this keep happening to me?

My night was ruined then. I didn't want to talk anymore. I just wanted to think and process what I'd just been told. It was then I had a flashback and realised which night it would have taken place.

It had been at our old hostel after we had fallen out (as we did every weekend when he had been drinking). I had finished work early that Friday night, so I got back to the hostel while Luca was still there, drinking with his mates. I said I wanted to go out with them, but he told me no. When I got upset and had a go at him, he put his hand up to my face to dismiss me, then walked away.

In the hostel, I bumped into Loo, and she asked if I was okay. I told her what had happened, and some other girls overheard and invited me out with them. Loo had said she would come, too, and she seemed happy about it. I continued to tell her how sad Luca made me and how worthless I felt because I was never good enough for him. The only time I made him happy was when I was giving him sex. Anything outside of that, he criticised me. Loo seemed to understand and told me I could do so much better than him and I should finish with him. She then said she would be back in a bit to go out with us girls, and she left, but she didn't come back. She never met us for a drink, and nobody knew where she was, which felt odd.

That night, I had a dream that Luca was with another woman. I woke up in the night with deep anxiety in my stomach. Within seconds of waking, I heard footsteps in the corridor outside my room and had an overwhelmingly strong urge to check on who it was. I actually trembled a little as I opened the bedroom door.

The only light in the corridor at that time of night was the fire exit sign, and I could see that Loo's bedroom door was open. As I walked down the corridor towards the room, the door was closing as if someone had just walked into the room, and I managed to see into the bedroom as the door was about to close. The bedroom was dark. I didn't see who had walked in, so I carried on down the corridor to the toilets. On my way back to my room a few minutes later, I glanced over at Loo's door, and I had this weird feeling that something wasn't right. Once back in bed, I agonised over where Luca might be and what he was doing. I hated the weekends because they were always the same: me in bed alone, wondering where he was.

Just minutes later, I heard a bedroom door open and a girl giggle, then footsteps walked down the corridor and disappeared. By that point, I was so heavily weighed down with misery that I didn't bother to get up to check if it was Luca, as I suspected. The girls sharing a room with Loo were the ones who always asked me what was happening between Luca and I and if we were serious, so I wouldn't be surprised to learn that he had been in the bedroom with one of them.

At some point, I fell asleep and was awoken later when someone shouted Luca's name. I got up to look outside my bedroom door and saw him and Loo walking up the corridor—so that's where she was! She was supposed to be getting ready to go out with us girls hours ago, and yet there she was... with Luca!

I called him over to talk to me, and Loo followed. I instantly told her to fuck off and stop hanging around. I was in no mood to play nice with her. She turned around and walked out into the kitchen, and Luca and I started a heated debate over whose behaviour was worse that night; then he stormed off into the kitchen. As much as I hated that guy, I also feared his leaving me as I believed he was so much better than me, and I would never get a guy like him again, so I followed him.

I met him in the kitchen and apologised (even though I hated him and knew he didn't deserve it), and I begged him to come back to bed with me. As this was going on, Loo was hovering in the dark at the back door of the kitchen, watching us. Looking back now, I think she was waiting for him, and they were obviously planning on spending the night together as it was 3 a.m. at that point, and there was nowhere to go out drinking. I'm glad she was standing there, though, because she got to witness my asking Luca to come back with me and watch Luca take my hand and walk off with me back to my bedroom, leaving her there alone in the kitchen. That was probably the only time that guy had chosen me!

When Clare told me that Luca and Loo had kissed, I'd assumed it was that night, but honestly, who knows? The morning after Clare broke the news to me, I went on Facebook to message Loo to ask if it was true. She replied, admitting they had kissed. She said she was sorry and that she felt it was wrong.

I felt compelled to ask if they had slept together. She said, 'Yes, we had sex before I left. I felt bad because he told me you were not together anymore. It didn't mean anything. I was really drunk and stupid.'

I thanked her for her honesty, then said I thought she was a fucking bitch and a cheap slut.

I was fuming. I'm actually glad I found out while I was in New Zealand and she was in Sweden because if we were still in the same hostel, I'd be taking a pair of scissors to her long blonde hair—I was THAT angry!

I then messaged Luca, telling him what I knew and reminding him of the times he'd said that if he found out I was with another guy, he would punch me in the face. I was furious and told him that if I were in Perth now, I'd stab him in the neck.

His reply was, 'Sorry. Tell Clare to go suck her father.' he was angrier at Clare for telling me about what he had been up to behind my back, than checking if I was ok.

This couldn't continue. I had allowed it to go on for so long, perceiving him to be someone he really wasn't, and I was becoming someone I didn't want to be. The aggression and anger were destructive and dangerous. I needed to take the blinkers off and see what was in front of me. He would never be the person I wanted him to be! I was lying to myself, which, in turn, kept me focused on someone who was also lying to me. Life continuously showed me what that guy was really like and pushed me to break away from him. If I had done that from the first or second time I had been shown the signs, it would have saved me from months of more pain and stress. Instead, I ignored the signs and carried on, and each subsequent sign was harder to deal with.

It's a universal law that if you're on the wrong path, life will gently nudge you off it, and if you ignore this, then something big will happen to FORCE you onto a different path. This was an almighty shove off the path, with a slap around the face for added effect.

It's also true that you will find things out when you are ready to receive them. I was definitely ready to receive that news when I did because, by that point, I had got over his leaving me for that other girl. This was because it wasn't serious between them, and according to my friend in Perth, he was spiteful to her and about her behind her back. She had cried to my friend one night, saying how horrible Luca treated her (I know how she felt, there!). So, Luca and I had reached a place of peace and were arranging to see each other in Perth. That was when life intervened and booted me off that path. His betrayal was revealed to me less than two weeks before Rachel and I headed back to Perth—perfect timing, really.

CHAPTER 14

The Tower Is Crumbling

In Tarot, the 'Tower Moment' is when life intervenes and knocks your tower down, making space for you to create something with a stronger foundation. My tower was beginning to crumble.

When Rachel and I returned to Perth, we decided not to go back to our old hostel and start afresh in a different one, run by the boyfriend of our friend Angela. Because it was in a backpacker area, I often ran into Luca and his newest girlfriend in bars and clubs. The first night he saw me out, he texted, saying, 'Don't fuck any of my friends,' then watched me all night, causing an argument between him and his girlfriend.

Another night out in a club, when a really hot guy was trying it on with me, Luca came over and tried to dance with me. His girlfriend wasn't out that night, so he was free to act like the arsehole he really was. He stuck to me all night, kissing and dancing with me. Then, at the end of the night, he asked me to go home with him, but I said no. He was puzzled why

I turned him down, so I reminded him of all the bullshit he'd done to me. He still didn't understand why it meant we couldn't have sex. This was not surprising, really—narcissists never see what they have done wrong, nor can they comprehend why someone doesn't want to be with them. For ages, he wouldn't accept what I was saying, and then, when it finally sank in, he left—no word, no explanation; he just left.

I also discovered around that time that he'd attacked the girl he'd finished with me for. He'd left her with bruises and bite marks all over her arms. It was hardly surprising, given that he'd done a similar thing to me with the biting. Let's face the facts: he was a bully. It took me a long time, but I finally saw him for what he was. The way he treated the other two girls was similar to how he treated me. He blamed me for everything, and for a long time, I believed him because of my low self-esteem. Now I know that he was the one with the problem, and he was a very damaged little boy.

During that time, I was overwhelmed with anxiety every day. I ignored and abandoned my needs, I pitied myself, I felt sad, worthless, not good enough and rejected. I believed that if I kept my thoughts positive, then this would all magically change how I felt, but of course, it didn't. In Luca and other external influences (i.e., other men and alcohol), I was searching to make myself feel good again. The more I continued on that destructive path, the worse my external world became. I was in and out of jobs like cleaning, waitressing and retail. None of them had full-time hours, none of them provided a friendly working environment, and none of them made me feel good.

Because of my lack mindset, the lack of work, money and optimism closely followed. I was so broke I couldn't afford my hostel any longer, so I had to clean it every morning in exchange for a night's board. I was going to food banks to eat, sharing food with friends at the hostel or just going hungry. When I did have money, I went to Coles Supermarket and bought either a peach or a plum for breakfast. I was having such a tough time. I honestly felt as if my life was on a downward spiral, and I just couldn't control anything that was happening to me.

One night, a cockroach crawled over my duvet when I was in bed, and I didn't even flinch. I just stared at it. Normally, I would have screamed and jumped out of bed, but I felt so heavy with negative emotions that I couldn't be bothered to react to it. I'd invested so much energy reacting to the other cockroach named Luca that I didn't have anything in me to react to this small creature. I just didn't care about anything at that point. I focused on this negativity and allowed the negative emotions to consume me, which ultimately made everything progressively worse over the next two months until the next event happened.

Luca left Australia. I was devastated and felt lost (which was odd, given that I hadn't been with him for months), but I felt 'lost' because I had invested my focus and energy into him, feeding off him, essentially, and now my 'source' had gone. Now, I needed to focus on myself, and that just seemed too daunting. I tried to keep positive thoughts, but they just weren't coming. How could they when my emotions were so negative? I'd spent months trying to do this, and all I'd manifested was more lack and misery. I had this feeling of unfairness. How did he get to jet off with his new girlfriend and be happy when he treated me like shit? Where was the karma in that? What was fair about that? How come shit people got good rewards? The way he treated all three of us girls was poor. He'd definitely cheated on all three of us, and I know he hit at least two of us, so why did he deserve to be happy?

Looking back, I realise that we three girls were extremely jealous of each other because we all knew what Luca was capable of, and we all knew he couldn't be trusted around other women. He lacked compassion, empathy, respect and emotional intelligence. Therefore, he'd never made any of us feel safe or secure with him. He had a dismissive/avoidant attachment style and literally dismissed or avoided any form of emotion. The three of us were all insecure and lacked self-esteem. That was the only reason we all wanted to be chosen by that boy, to feel wanted, worthy and good enough. If we loved ourselves enough to choose ourselves, there was no way any of us would have remained with him. He was not a nice person. He had far too much unresolved trauma of his own that made him incapable of loving anyone, including himself. Secure people with self-respect never treat others the way he treated us. Initially, I thought I'd made him treat me so badly because I wasn't good enough to be with someone on his level. It was only after finding out he'd treated those other girls the same way he had me that I knew HE was the common denominator, yet he happily allowed us to believe we were the problem, and we'd made him treat us like shit.

Once I'd finally allowed myself to see the truth of who he was, I had a lot of guilt and shame directed at myself for allowing it to happen to me. I had gone from hating myself for not being good enough to feeling ashamed of myself, and although I moved on from Luca and had other relationships in the future, the feelings of not being good enough and shame were still active. I just wasn't aware they were there as they had become so normal to feel that they were interwoven in the fabric of my being and became my predominant feelings.

This affected all my future relationships/situationships, as I entered all of them with the idea that I wasn't good enough to receive a healthy relationship, and whatever happened between us would always be centred around my feeling ashamed of myself and my behaviour. So, once again, I was building a new tower on an already unstable, rotten foundation, and it was only a matter of time before life knocked it back down.

I blamed myself for everything surrounding this. I know that taking accountability for your actions is the best way to heal; however, I took on the responsibility for things that were not mine to carry. I overcompensated, taking on Luca's problems and making them mine. I now realise which ones were his and which were mine and have released myself from his burdens, energetically launching them back at him. I have learnt that people project their issues onto others instead of resolving them themselves. Once you take the time to heal and become more self-aware, you will be able to successfully differentiate between what is yours to deal with and What is someone else's harmful projections.

I don't know what Luca is doing now, nor do I care. I do hope, though, that he has grown and learnt how to treat his girlfriends better.

As for the two girls he was with in Perth, I hope they have found the love, respect and security they deserve and that they are happy.

CHAPTER 15

The Tower Has Fallen

My tower had been torn down from its parasitic, rotten foundation, and I was now ready to rebuild it with more secure roots.

Once Luca had left and I could no longer feed off his negative energy, I had the free space to create something better. I decided to take a break on the East Coast of Australia to recalibrate. I needed to do something different so I could create different results. Things were not going to improve if I continued to repeat what I had been doing the last few months. It was time to take responsibility and change my circumstances. I also felt like going alone, so I didn't ask anyone to come with me. I booked my flight to Brisbane and planned to travel up the coast to Cairns by using the Greyhound coach. Then, I booked a flight from Cairns to Alice Springs before going back to Perth. In total, I planned to be gone for one month, and boy, did I need it!

Spending a month away by myself did wonders for my well-being. I was able to start anew. I had never been to the East Coast before, so I didn't have any memories there to reflect upon. I could be whoever I wanted to be. I actually made friends with people I met along the way up the coast, as I would generally bump into the same people journeying up and visiting the same places as me. This was really refreshing, as I was spending time with people who had no connection to anyone I knew, and it was like starting a new chapter. I'm not going to lie, it was scary going over there by myself, not knowing the places or the people, but I went anyway. I didn't allow the fear to stand in my way. I had gone to Australia to travel, so that's exactly what I was going to do. More than that, I needed peace, and I wasn't getting it in Perth.

When I returned to Perth a month later, I was completely transformed. I felt good, fulfilled, optimistic and confident. This time around, I knew I was going to get a good job with full time hours in a nice working environment and make lots of money. I also knew I was going to live somewhere better and meet different people.

One of my friends said I could stay at his for free until I'd found a job, and then I could start paying rent. I moved in and set about job hunting. This time, I felt so optimistic about it, unlike the last time, when I continuously felt shit, and therefore, landed shit jobs. Within a week of returning from the East Coast, I got a waitressing job in a fine dining restaurant with full-time hours and a decent hourly rate; I loved it! My colleagues were great, the customers were generous tippers, and it was within walking distance of my new home, so there were no transport costs. I really enjoyed my job, so I was happy to take overtime, and I made fantastic friendships there. The money just began rolling in so fast, and I had so much disposable income. I could finally go to the hairdressers for the first time in a year and a half of being in Australia. Up until that point, I'd been cutting my hair over the bin with regular scissors from the kitchen. I could also buy clothes and shoes. I could buy food for breakfast that wasn't a can of cold peas or a plum. I could pay rent for a room instead of cleaning the hostel in exchange for a bed. I was literally bossing it! I was finally making money rather than having to steal it.

One of the jobs I had before going to the East Coast was run in a way that made it easy for me to steal money. That was definitely not my proudest moment, but I was desperate. I was broke and couldn't see any way out of my situation. One of my friends was an exotic dancer making lots of money, and her boss offered me a job. I really didn't want to do it—absolutely no judgement on the girls that do. My friend and her colleagues were the loveliest girls ever, and they were rolling in the money they needed to get them through college, university, raising kids or travelling. I just didn't want to do it and decided to find another way, which was to steal.

I had to do this carefully over a few months and not do anything stupid to attract attention and get found out. When I eventually had enough, I used the money to buy my flight to the East Coast. I'm so sorry to my boss, but I was desperate.

I can see how people are tricked and exploited when they are broke. That's when the hyenas and vultures come out to feed on the vulnerable. My friend's boss wasn't the only one to offer me a job. I met many old men, rich men, who wanted me to 'spend time' with them. Gross.

I was lucky in my first year in Australia as my mum and brother lent me money if I needed it, but in my second year, I really didn't want to keep asking them. It just wasn't an option for me.

So, I was now back in Perth with my new job, new income and new home, feeling new and fresh. A couple months after I was back, a Welsh girl called Jayne moved into the spare room of the house I was at. We became friends, and she is now one of my best friends. As we are both back in the UK, we meet up regularly in England and Wales.

I'm so grateful for the time away on the East Coast because it enabled me to recalibrate, get my life back on track, make money to rent the room and ultimately, meet Jayne.

So, while I managed to manifest my finances, home and social life, I still hadn't fully addressed the trauma bonds that kept me stuck in toxic relationships, believing I belonged at the bottom of the barrel. The results of this became evident when B entered my life.

CHAPTER 16
B Is for Bullshit

B was a Tunisian guy who'd come to Australia to sell drugs. I was friends with his brother, who had since gone back to France. My friend asked if B could stay with me until he found his feet. B had arrived in Australia with just $80 in his pocket and a plethora of fantasies in his head. He and his brother genuinely thought B was going to go to Perth, sell drugs to backpackers and get rich. He tried and failed spectacularly at selling drugs and getting rich in his own country, so why he thought he could make a success of it in Australia just blew my mind. Anyway, when I first met him, I liked him and enjoyed having him around. He was polite and sweet and wanted to go out socialising with me a lot (basically, he was everything Luca wasn't). We soon started sleeping with each other, and for a moment, I was happy. That was until B lost his wallet and passport one night.

The next day, a girl messaged me on Facebook, saying she was B's girlfriend and that she would transfer money for him into my account.

Excuse me? His what? He told me he had split from his girlfriend three months earlier. I confronted him about this, and he said she wasn't his girlfriend —and yet there she was, sending him money. I didn't speak to him for the rest of the day and made him sleep on the sofa.

The next morning, he said he had finished with her (after accepting her money), and he wanted to be with me. I really was not fussed at that point—I didn't want him anymore. He was far too weak and could not make decisions about anything, always relying on me to tell him what to do and agreeing with everything I said, not having his own opinion. I found it frustrating because it was not genuine, and he didn't show me his real personality. B said he wanted us to make a go of things, and my intuition screamed at me to get rid of him, but my behavioural pattern was such that I ignored it. I still had a low opinion of myself and believed I wasn't good enough to be with a decent guy. That's what prompted me to take up his offer. I mean, he was still a step up from Luca, after all. At least B wanted to be seen with me in public, and he included me in his social activities.

Very quickly, I started to notice that B's 'ex' kept calling him. One night, we were at the pub for a couple of hours, and she kept calling him the entire time, and he wouldn't pick up. He told me, 'She's crazy,' and that she wanted him back. It was such a lazy cop-out to call a girl crazy as a way to assassinate her character when she isn't conforming to what you want. That was exactly what was going on there. They were obviously still together, so I told him that when I returned from Bali, he needed to move out (I was due to go to Bali in a couple of days for a week). I asked him again if they were still together, and he denied it, so I told him to tell me the truth, or I would message her and ask.

The arrogant asshole smirked at me—the game was on.

'Seriously, do NOT test or underestimate me!!' I typed out the message on Facebook while he watched. Then, I showed him the message and said he had one last chance before I pressed send. He smirked at me again, and I pressed send.

His facial expression went into a state of panic, his mouth open, his eyes wide, and he finally admitted that they were still together. I don't know if it was from being ultra thick or very arrogant that he'd choose to drag his secret out to the last second before telling me the truth, but he learnt very quickly that I didn't make empty threats. He then had the audacity to say, 'Are you happy to have started a war? I didn't think you were like that.'

The girlfriend texted back, confirming that B was her boyfriend and asking why I wanted to know. I told her to speak with him, which was a huge mistake. It highlighted how I chose other people's feelings over my own because I didn't want to get him into trouble, so I thought if he explained, it would be better for him. And it was better for him, but definitely not for me. He told her he had met me three times at a party, that I wanted him, but he wasn't interested, and I was crazy.

What?

She then texted, calling me a bitch and a whore, so I told her he was living with me and he had told me he was single.

She didn't even bother to ask me any questions to clarify anything. She immediately took his side without question. I understand living in denial, but I would have interrogated all parties involved to try to find any gaps in the story.

I'd started off feeling sorry for her, but when I realised she wasn't even going to ask me for my side of the story, I quickly changed my mind.

Fuck her. The way he'd acted so brazenly with me indicated this was not his first rodeo. He'd clearly been unfaithful before, and if this was how she reacted to it, then she was enabling him, so I didn't care about her feelings or his. They deserved each other.

He spent the entire next day in the garden with his tail between his legs, only coming in to ask if I had any darks I wanted going in the wash.

After I finished work that night, the girlfriend texted me, saying I was a bitch and causing trouble. What the hell was she doing messaging me? This annoyed me, so I told her that I had told him to move out, so she should shut the fuck up. I then explained that he had been with me at my house the previous night when all of this kicked off, and I had NOT met him three times at a party.

A few minutes after sending her that message, B texted called me a bitch, and said that I was playing games with his life and that he was gonna fuck my life up every day.

I was nervous on my way home from work, thinking he was either going to rob me or be physically aggressive to me. Once home, he looked furious and began shouting at me, calling me a bitch because I'd made his girlfriend cry.

Now, I was pissed off, and the nerves had disappeared— I'd made her cry? This had nothing at all to do with his infidelity and lies? I shouted at him, stepped towards him and pointed my finger in his face. He told me not to do that, but I'd lost it by that point. He blamed me for how his girlfriend felt after all he'd done? The dickhead had crawled his way into my life, made moves on me, told me he was single and had plenty of chances to tell me the truth. He was so arrogant that he'd actually watched me type the message out to his girlfriend and just sat there, smirking at me.

As I was shouting at him, I felt my anger gain momentum and felt like lashing out, so I quickly turned around and walked off.

He calmly asked me to stay and not to message her anymore. I calmly told him I wouldn't, but if she reached out to me, I'd reply. I showed him the messages she had sent me so he saw for himself that I wasn't going out of my way to tell her stories. I was just reacting to her calling me names.

When I got into bed, she texted, calling me a whore (again), so I responded.

As if by magic, a few seconds later, B came into my bedroom, shaking his head at me. I said, 'She texted me first,' and showed him my phone. That cheeky bitch had been telling him that I was randomly texting her stuff, leaving out the part where she'd contacted me first to call me names. Now that he had been shown proof of what was actually happening, he apologised and went back to the garden to smoke weed and tell more lies to his girlfriend.

It was short-lived, as she soon came back, threatening me if I didn't stay away from B.

Oh, no—too far, honey. Too far. She couldn't threaten me.

I told her that B was with me right then, sitting in my garden and still living with me. That girl had done nothing but verbally abuse me and blame everything on me. I warned B to tell her the truth or tell her to leave me alone because each time she sent me a shitty message, I vowed to disclose more information to her about him and me. At that point, I hadn't yet told her he had asked to be my boyfriend, but that card was going to be played soon enough.

A few minutes later, B came back to my room to have a go at me, but I showed him the messages, and he finally said he would tell her the truth. His 'truth', however, was that he had tried to chat me up but nothing happened between us.

Bloody hell! He was just incapable of telling the truth!

He alleged she'd finished with him after hearing that. He seemed upset for a whole two minutes before asking if it was finished between him and me. Of course it was! Honestly, the audacity blows my mind! That guy was incredibly thick!

Not accepting that as an answer, he tried to have sex with me, but he was immediately shut down and told to get out of my room. I then placed my desk in front of the door as a barrier.

I arrived in Bali, excited to see Lucy. It was so lovely to see her again. I had missed her so much. She was one of those friends you just feel safe and peaceful with. She was one of the first people I could be vulnerable with in my life and talk about how I actually felt rather than how I told myself I felt.

We were due to spend seven days there before I returned to Australia, and she returned to Belgium. We used the week to explore the island, staying in different hostels and using taxis as our mode of transportation to each of the different places. On our fifth day, we were drinking beer in the beach bar, discussing where we wanted to go next and searching for a hostel to stay at that night. We were typical backpackers. We didn't worry about making rigid plans but just took each day as it came and decided there and then where we would move to next and sort out accommodation on that same day.

Just as we had agreed upon where we would go next, a taxi pulled up and dropped off an elderly couple, so we approached the driver and asked if he could take us to our next destination. He said he would be back in twenty minutes, to which I replied that it was too soon, as our bags were still at our hostel. The driver, named Ben, assured us he would take us back to the hostel to collect our things and advised that we relax and finish our beer. It was great because it worked out perfectly … or so we thought.

Shortly after the driver left, a man approached us, saying that Ben had sent him to take us on his behalf as he couldn't do the two-hour drive to our next destination. That was fine as we were just super excited for our next adventure, but from the moment we got into the man's car, something felt 'off'. My stomach felt a little nervous. It was completely different from how it had felt a few moments before.

On the short drive to our hostel, the man was really nice and chatty, but there was something that didn't feel right to the point that when we checked out of the hostel, I told the manager where we were going and that if we didn't make it, the driver was responsible for our disappearance. I had said this in front of the driver, too, and he just laughed it off. I have never felt the need to make a remark like that, but something prompted me to do so this particular time.

The driver put our bags into the back of the car, and I got in but very reluctantly. Once he drove off, I began to feel sad and a bit nervous. It was a huge shift from the excitement and eagerness I had felt less than an hour before when we were planning our next adventure. I thought that if I got to know a little more about him I would be at ease, so I asked him questions, including if he'd been to Australia before. He said, 'No, I wish.' He then claimed that he had been to England and Belgium after Lucy and I told him where we were from.

It was odd. Australia was a couple of hours' flight from Bali. He'd never been, even though he wished he had, but he'd somehow been to England and Belgium, which were both on the other side of the world, a long-haul flight away? That did not make me feel good at all. This guy was not legit, and now, my anxiety accelerated. I looked over to Lucy, who had her head led against the window, her eyes closed. How could she be so calm when I was a nervous wreck? This was normally the point where I would see that someone else was okay and call myself stupid for overreacting and reading the situation wrong, but this time, my intuition took over my self-critical thoughts. I couldn't sit still, and my breathing was rapid and shallow.

I looked around the car and noticed there was no ID at the front of the car like the previous taxi drivers I'd had. I also noticed that the man was very well dressed and dripping in gold, unlike the other taxi drivers we'd had so far. I then suddenly realised that the BMW SUV was also unlike any of the cars we had gotten into before, so I asked him the question I should have asked before I got into the car with him: 'Are you actually a taxi driver working for Ben or just his friend?'

He replied, 'I'm Ben's friend. He asked me to pick you up.'

At that moment, I realised we had been duped into getting into a car with a stranger. It was not a taxi! My stomach now swirled with fear. My heart pounded in my chest. My body was frozen. My mind suddenly realised what my body was trying to tell me the whole time. From the moment we got into the man's car, my intuition had notified me that something wasn't right. My impulse was to tell the hostel manager that if something happened to Lucy and me it was down to this driver. It came from a genuine place of knowing something was not right. The fear, anxiety and unsettledness I continued to feel in the car despite the man's friendliness was my intuition warning me to get away from that situation.

At that point of stark realisation, the man dropped the bomb that we would be picking up some of his friends and going to a 'party together' somewhere in the jungle. That was all I needed to understand that we had been tricked and were not being taken to where we had told Ben we wanted to go.

I told the man we didn't want to go to a party, that we wanted to go to our new hostel, where our boyfriends were waiting for us (the classic lie girls tell when they feel unsafe). He wouldn't listen and kept on that we would have a "great party" with plenty of alcohol.

I asked him how he'll take us to our hostel if he'll be drinking, to which he said that we would stay the night at the party and he would drive us back tomorrow.

Now, I started to feel sick. I couldn't breathe properly, and I heard and felt the blood pounding in my ears and my heart banging in my chest. I woke up Lucy and told her what the man had said. She, too, pleaded with him to take us to our hostel and not to any party, but he was adamant that we were going to the party because it had already been arranged, and we were on our way to pick up his friends. By that point, it seemed as if we were already in the jungle as we were surrounded by trees and nothing else.

Upon continuing to plead with the man not to take us to his party, he changed his story slightly to say that a woman would be joining us, and we could sit with her. Of course, we didn't believe him and repeated that we didn't want to go.

I had sat in the back and had my hands wrapped tightly around the headrest of the front passenger's seat, sitting on the end of my seat, leaning into the gap between the front passenger's and driver's seats, telling the man we didn't want to go to his party. My body was so pumped with adrenaline from fear that I couldn't sit still, and I couldn't breathe properly. I had no idea where we were or where we were going. I just knew that nobody in the whole world would know where to find us or even that we had gone missing. The mobile phone I had back then was one without the Internet, just a bog-standard phone that made calls and sent text messages, so I couldn't WhatsApp anyone my location (that was even if I had access to the Internet). I felt so helpless, and I couldn't think straight as my body was awash with fear and anxiety.

Thank the Lord that, at some point, the man pulled over somewhere. To be honest, I can't remember if he went to get a friend or he went into a shop. I really don't remember why he stopped the car exactly, but he got out, and I expressed my concerns to Lucy about how I had felt the entire time, even before he mentioned going to a party. She suggested I call Ben, so I did.

I told Ben that his friend was going to take us to a party, but we didn't want to go, and we asked if he could send us another driver. Ben responded, 'Why don't you just go to the party with him?'

My jaw dropped to the floor. This asshole was in on it too! This was a total setup!

After freezing and a moment's silence, I firmly told Ben that we didn't want to go. He sighed at me and hung up.

I was shocked. Lucy was shocked. The depth of the situation had become very clear: we needed to get out, and now!

We rushed to the boot of the car to grab our things before the man came back. I got my bag out and heard the man shout, 'Hey, what are you doing?' as he ran over and stood in front of the boot of the car, preventing Lucy from getting her bag. I told him we were leaving as we didn't want to go to a party with him and his friends, so he came up with the bright idea of just the three of us going. For goodness' sake--they certainly missed him when the persuasion and negotiation skills were being given out.

I said, 'No,' again, and this went back and forth for a while before Lucy said, 'Get out my way,' and shoved him to the side to grab her bag. He was five-foot fuck-all and skinny, so he wasn't too hard to push out of the way.

Once we both had our bags, we ran off in the direction we had come from. Although, when I say 'run', we were both wearing flip-flops, so that was very hard to do. We had no idea where we were other than in the jungle, perhaps, and we both expected the man or one of his friends to pull up and snatch us. The fear and adrenaline kept us running despite the lack of suitable footwear and heavy bags.

Thankfully, it didn't take too long before we saw two women standing outside a wooden hut. The sight of those women filled me with comfort. We ran over to them, out of breath, heightened anxiety, stumbling over our words to tell them what had just happened. I know that, in movies, you sometimes see an escapee seek shelter in a home that turns out to be linked to the captor, and quite honestly, throwing myself at the nearest people and going into their property is not something I advise. However, in this case, at the time, we didn't have the capacity to think clearly, and we didn't know where we were. We just saw two females and our unconscious bias made us feel as if we would be safe with them. We were lucky the women were decent people who wanted to help us.

One of the women told us that taxis did not come in BMW SUVs and that each time you got a taxi you had to fill in a form as part of the booking process. This was exactly the procedure we had done thus far, but as it was not part of our normal process, we didn't catch on to the fact that every taxi journey should start that way.

The woman called us a taxi, and we waited at her place for it to arrive. I was so nervous and on-edge by that point that I repeatedly asked her if she had booked a legitimate taxi.

When the taxi arrived, it was a beat-up old car, not a flash BMW. The driver was not dripping in gold or wearing designer clothes. His ID was displayed in the car, and we filled out a form before he took us. It was a genuine taxi. Finally!

We both hugged the women (our saviours), asked one more time if it was a legitimate taxi, then got in and headed off. I was still anxious and couldn't relax on the journey at all. I sat up stiff, wide-eyed, and looked around for any signs of being followed by a white BMW SUV.

This scenario is the best example I can give of the power of intuition. From the time I got into that car, my intuition immediately told me it wasn't safe, and it manifested itself in my body. My stomach swirled with nerves and unease, my heart raced, and my breathing was shallow, yet minutes before, I had been happy and relaxed in the bar, excited to go on our next trip. Even the fact that I'd told the hostel manager that if something happened to us, the driver would be responsible for our disappearance, and that was before he told us about the party.

We all have intuition inside of us. We just need to understand what it is and the clues our bodies give us. I didn't understand what happened to me then, and I relied upon logic over feelings. If that were to happen now, I would listen to the clues in my body right from the start. I have genuinely never felt so terrified in my entire life. I think about all of the people who have been victims of kidnapping or similar crimes, and my heart goes out to them because Lucy and I had a brief encounter, and we escaped. I can't begin to understand the fear that goes through someone's body when they realise they're not going to escape from something like that.

Once settled into our new accommodation (which was a hotel, as we felt like treating ourselves after having such an awful time), we went out for a lot of strong drinks and reflected upon what had happened that day. We were finally beginning to feel safe again. That is until the next morning arrived.

My passport was stolen.

Lucy and I went for breakfast, and when we returned to our room, Lucy's handbag, which she had left on the floor, was now on her bed, open, her receipts out. She checked inside, and twenty Euros were missing. I checked my bag and noticed my passport, which I had left on top of all my clothes so it would be easier to find when we checked into another hostel that day, had gone missing. This sparked a four-hour stand-off with the receptionist at the hotel, as they said the manager wouldn't be able to meet me to discuss my 'problem', so I waited until he did.

I refused to leave and requested they search their staff as I knew my passport and Lucy's money were there before we left for breakfast. The receptionist got the manager on the phone to talk to me, and he questioned if we had 'misplaced' our items, assuring us that none of his staff would steal.

I told him they obviously did because we were missing a passport and some money.

He said he didn't know what time he would be back, but I waited, regardless. At that time, I called the British Embassy to tell them I had a flight back to Australia the next day and had a job to go to, so I really needed my passport. Unfortunately, they couldn't provide me with an alternative for a few days.

I was in such a panic. I thought I would be stuck there, alone, as Lucy was leaving, too. After what had happened the previous day and now this, I was in a heightened state of anxiety and not feeling well at all.

Once the manager arrived, he took us to an empty room to discuss where we had gone and when we had last seen our items. I told him we had packed our bags right before going to the dining room for breakfast as we were going to check out afterwards. We were gone for roughly thirty minutes, and when we returned, some cleaners were outside the room next door, and our room had been cleaned.

Upon hearing this, he went off for about twenty minutes. When he returned, he had another man with him and asked if he could look through my bag. I agreed he could because

I had nothing to hide. Both of the men huddled over the bag with their backs to me so I couldn't see my bag. This unnerved me—why wouldn't they open up my bag and let me see what they were doing inside it? Finding this all very suspicious, I got up out of my seat and walked briskly over to the corner of the room, where they were carrying out this secretive operation, and said firmly, 'What are you doing?'

In an instant, the manager pulled my passport out of what I can only describe as 'thin air'. He claimed he had just found it in my bag. As if! The bag was tiny, and I had already spent four hours emptying it and putting it back together again.

You know what? I just accepted it because I was just so grateful to have my passport back, and I just wanted to leave. I felt a surge of relief and slumped down into my chair, exhaling all the stress that had been accumulating inside of me.

Lucy then asked about her money. She invited the manager to search through her bag, too. The manager agreed he would, but he sent the other man away, and he looked through her bag in a completely different manner than what he had done to mine. He pulled her bag to the middle of the room, sat beside it and pulled everything out, allowing us clear visibility of what he was doing. This solidified our suspicions that one of his cleaners had stolen my passport and he had planted it back in my bag.

He calmly searched through Lucy's bag whilst chatting with us. Of course, he didn't find the money because the cleaner had stolen it. Lucy knew she wouldn't get it back, and it wasn't as important as a passport, so we didn't pursue it any further. We just left and took a legitimate taxi to our next hostel, where we remained vigilant about all of our belongings.

As if that wasn't enough, B's girlfriend text me that night whilst we were out having our goodbye dinner and called me a whore. Who knows why? I had told him to move out of my home, so maybe she was just overthinking and winding herself up over it. By that point, I had lost any sympathy for her.

Lucy took my phone and argued with the girl in French, pretending to be me. That was much faster than me having to Google Translate everything. Lucy is like me. She has a very sharp tongue when needed, and she did such a good job of destroying that girl, that she gave up and stopped texting me.

Lucy and I agreed that it was always eventful wherever I went. I reflected upon that on my plane journey back to Australia in a victim-like manner, wondering why nothing peaceful ever happened for me. I now realise it was because my thoughts and feelings were so chaotic that I continuously manifested a chaotic lifestyle.

I returned to Australia with a deep sense of anxiety—from the near-miss kidnapping, the stolen passport, and now having to go back and deal with whatever shit B had in store for me. I really thought he would still be hanging around like a bad smell. Turns out he left! He went to a hostel. Amazing!

After a few days of peace, he texted, asking to borrow $100! I refused to do it because of the way he had treated me, so he called me a big shit and a bitch, said he hated me, he never wanted to see my face again, he regretted ever meeting me, he didn't need a girl like me and that I disgusted him.

I didn't bother replying. I didn't care about him or his opinion.

When he realised I wasn't going to respond, he texted to tell me he missed me, and he understood why I didn't want to talk to him anymore, so he'd delete my number and leave me alone.

He didn't delete my number, though, because he texted me a few days later after 72g of cocaine had been posted to my house from France. The absolute bellend had it delivered to mine, and my housemate signed for it.

The four of us opened it up and tried a bit. It was crap, but we decided we would sell it and split the money as a form of compensation for having B disrupt our lives over the last six weeks. This seemed like a good idea until a silver Lexus pulled up outside my house, and an angry B jumped out and raced down the path. My housemate and I were sitting outside at the time. We ran inside, and B started pounding on the door, but we didn't answer. He kept calling me (on the number he said he was going to delete), but I didn't answer. He eventually left, but for the rest of the day, the Lexus kept crawling slowly past my house and occasionally parked right outside. Luckily, I was off work that day, so I didn't need to go outside and be caught by him, but I couldn't keep it up forever.

B texted to say he knew we had the drugs as he had seen online that Jayne had signed for the package. There was literally no point in keeping the cocaine. B had been drug trafficking for years. He was dumb as shit, but he knew what he was doing with that, and he knew I had it. So, after a good 11-hour standoff, I let him have the drugs on the condition that whoever was in the car did not come into the house. He agreed and came into the house alone. He even gave me $200 for the inconvenience!

Reflecting on that time in my life makes me feel incredibly grateful for the peace I have in my life now. I don't have a lot of stories or dramatic events to talk about anymore, and that's because I have peace now. It's so refreshing having nothing to complain about. I've created this peace in my life simply by setting boundaries, putting myself first and listening to my intuition. I'd done none of those things around the time B had come into my life. He'd have never had even a minute of my life if I had those things already in place. We all have the tools to do this. The tools I implemented didn't have a significant impact initially, but they definitely started me on the right path and encouraged me to practice yoga, meditation and reiki.

It has now been over a year since I started practising being present after following the guidance of Eckhart Tolle in *The Power Of Now*, remaining in the present moment, transmuting negative feelings and watching negative thoughts but not identifying or attaching myself with them. This dissolves any negative feelings, and I can go back to being calm and balanced again. This has been the most transformative part of my healing, and it has worked faster than anything else for me.

Although I can now preach about how important it is to allow your emotions to be your internal compass, I still hadn't learnt that lesson after my time with B, and I continued to listen to my anxious, belittling thoughts. My thoughts, by default, were chaotic, so that was what I continued to attract into my life, and the cycle continued.

CHAPTER 17

Recalibration in the Riviera

In December 2014, my working holiday visa expired, and I had to return to England. My friends threw me a surprise leaving party and showered me with gifts. I felt so loved and supported by each and every one of them. The friendships I made in Australia were significantly better than any friendships I had back at home. This was because, in Australia, I was away from people telling me who I was, how I should behave and what I should do. At home, I had yielded to other people's opinions of me and adopted their perceptions as my truth. In Australia, I was free from this, and I had ample opportunity to be myself. I was never fully authentically myself, though, as I hadn't done any real healing work. However, because I was in a different environment, surrounded by different people, I had fewer restrictions on myself, and naturally, had a different mindset and, in turn, made different choices. These choices were based more on what I wanted to do and not what others suggested I do. I deliberately and gradually changed my vibrational frequency, and this allowed me to grow and discover more about who I was at my core.

After leaving Australia, I went over to France in 2015 and worked as an au pair, where I learnt how to speak French. This was an interesting experience, and one I am grateful for as it helped me believe I was capable of doing anything I put my mind to. When I arrived in France, I couldn't speak French, but by the time I left, I was able to have a conversation about politics. Even in English, that subject is difficult to talk about.

I was based in the south of France, in a gorgeous area called Antibes. The house was gorgeous, with traditional wooden shutters you could close over the windows, on the top of a hill, looking down upon the forest below. We had a swimming pool there, so when the children had their midmorning nap, I could swim for a half hour and then have lunch before they woke up. It was such a beautiful, serene life, and one my soul required after the fast-paced, chaotic lifestyle I had led in Australia over the previous two years. I just enjoyed being with the kids, swimming and learning to speak French.

After a few months of enjoying my new life and feeling more relaxed with myself, I was given some time off, so I took myself out for the entire day. I went to Juan Les Pans and walked along the seafront, enjoying the warm sun on my face and body. I felt good about myself because my level of French had improved by that point, and I felt confident when speaking to people. Juan Les Pans is filled with beach bars, and I was deciding which one I wanted to go into when I saw the most incredible vision ever: a muscly, six-foot-five man with his top off setting up the DJ booth at a beach bar. He looked like a young Denzel Washington.

I had to go to that bar! Luckily for me, there were plenty of empty chairs near the DJ booth, so I could get as close to him as possible. In France, it is completely normal for women to be topless, so I whipped off my top, and within seconds, the sexy Denzel lookalike approached me and introduced himself as the manager. Upon ordering my drink with him, he recognised that I was English, so he began asking me why I was in France. After a little chat, he took my order for a glass of wine and went to collect it for me.

I relaxed in my chair, staring out at the beautiful sea, blissfully thinking how beautiful that man was when he appeared behind my right shoulder with my wine on a tray. As he leant down to place the tray in front of my face, I saw his eyes staring at my exposed tits, and he lost control of the tray, tipping it and spilling the glass of wine on my stomach. Feeling the shock of the cold wine, I immediately knocked the glass on the floor and jumped up. The glass smashed when it hit the floor, and I jumped directly on top of it, yelling out in pain as a shard sliced into my toe.

He was so apologetic and ran to get a pair of tweezers and a towel. I sat down, drying my torso as he held onto my foot and gently pulled the glass out of my toe.

And that was how I met Mario.

Mario was simply stunning... such a beautiful man. He allowed me to have the next drink for free (quite rightly), and he asked for my phone number as he wanted to see me again.

It turned out that he owned that particular bar and said that he was there seven days a week. He suggested I go back there to spend some time with him. I wasn't able to meet him for another week on my next day off, but he texted me every day up until that point.

On my next day off, Mario came to pick me up from mine. I will never forget the image of him when the electronic gates to the front of the house opened up slowly, and he was on the other side, leaning against his motorbike. The six-foot-five-inch machine, dressed in motorbike leathers, smiled at me. I swear, my knees wanted to buckle from underneath me. That vision of him and the motorbike embodied strength, power and masculinity. It was incredible, and unlike anything I had ever experienced before.

As beautiful and lovely as Mario was, I ended it before it really took off. Although he was everything I had ever wanted, I didn't feel safe with him. I wasn't used to successful, genuine men. I didn't know how to handle it, and I was in a state of high anxiety when I was around him because I felt so small, insignificant and worthless compared to him. He had everything, and I had nothing (or so I perceived back then). I felt he was too good for me and that it wouldn't last, so I should end it with him before he ended it with me. I felt as if I belonged with guys who had problems and needed fixing, guys with issues and unresolved trauma. Being with a healed, secure man only showed me how unhealed and insecure I was, and I didn't want to feel that way.

I'm not surprised I attracted Mario into my life because I had taken a few months by myself, focusing on the kids I was looking after, learning French and recalibrating, so after all that time working on myself, feeling good and refreshed, I'd attracted a man who fulfilled all of my requirements. However, because I hadn't pulled my trauma bonds out from their roots, it didn't take long for them to resurface and cause me to self-sabotage something I desired and deserved. Those feelings of unworthiness and insecurity I felt when I was with him should have been dealt with then. His presence in my life highlighted those unhealed parts of me I needed to work on but instead, I ran away from them and discarded him. I lost him because I didn't want to feel and heal those feelings. I began to question the efficiency of meditation, yoga and positive affirmations after that because it felt as if they were tools that had tricked me into believing I could achieve something better in my life, only to have it taken away as it didn't feel right.

Dr Joe Dispenza explains this belief perfectly. We can think positive thoughts and do conscious affirmations, but it is said that our consciousness only accounts for 5% of our brains. The other 95% is our unconscious brain. So, everything we experience and internalise crystalises itself into this part of our brain, repeating the same patterns, having the same triggers, behaving the same way, calling in the same people and calling in the same situations as in the past. The nervous system needs to be rewired.

The triggering of these negative feelings that surfaced when I was with Mario was my nervous system doing the job it had been accustomed to doing all my life. I had been developing consciously, but it had not penetrated my subconscious, and therefore, my nervous system had not been re-wired, and I was left acting out the same self-sabotaging patterns.

I know we shouldn't regret anything as each experience makes us who we are, however, I wish I hadn't rejected Mario. If I met him today, now that I'm much more healed and secure, I would keep hold of him and appreciate everything about him.

I stayed in France for a little under 12 months until I felt as if it was time to move on. Once I had achieved my goal of learning the language, I was ready for a new adventure.

Towards the end of 2015, Rachel suggested I get a tourist visa for three months and go to stay with her in Australia. I missed Australia, and I had got all I needed from my time in France, so I put the flight on my credit card and flew over to Perth. I wasn't allowed to work on a tourist visa, but I needed to pay my credit card off, so Rachel got me a job cleaning people's houses for cash in hand. This wasn't lucrative by any means, and I really didn't have many jobs coming in.

During my time at Rachel's, her husband's friend took a bit of a shine to me and wanted to take me out. The guy was funny, successful, rich, ambitious and kind, and he made a lot of effort to impress me, but I resisted. I was cold and uninviting to him. He made me feel uncomfortable. The truth is, he intimidated the shit out of me! I felt completely inferior to him and could not at all understand why he would want to be with someone like me. I literally had nothing to offer him, and I believed there was nothing about me that was worth pursuing. The qualities he possessed made me feel uncomfortable, and I responded by reacting negatively towards him. I had never before experienced what it was like to have a high-value man try to date me, and it was completely foreign to me. I felt as if I didn't belong there with him, and I certainly didn't feel as if he should be taking me out and paying for everything because that was not what I deserved. He never did anything wrong; it was me and my insecurities about myself, not anything about him.

Clearly, this never turned into a relationship. I was far too broken to have a healthy relationship with anyone. However, I am pleased to say that despite leaving Australia in December 2015, that man and I still occasionally talk via social media, and there are no hard feelings between us whatsoever. I am so grateful to him for showing me what it feels like to have a decent man who wants to be with me just as I am, without taking from me and trying to control, suppress or change me.

Those men do exist—I just needed to believe I was worthy of receiving them.

CHAPTER 18

Cruising, Caribbean & Chaos

After leaving Australia for the second time, I decided I was ready for another new adventure and landed myself a job on a cruise ship.

It was a horrible working environment: 18-hour days, getting paid for eight, money deducted from your wages if you were sick, no days off allowed and plenty of threats and intimidation from management. There was a rumour going around that cruise ships are a form of modern-day slavery, and I can tell you that's not far from the truth. Exploitation was rife on my ship, and apparently, I was working for one of the nicest companies. As a woman, I was treated appallingly by a lot of the men, especially by those I wouldn't have sex with. Once I'd said no, they were really spiteful, called me names and criticised my looks (looks that hadn't bothered them when they'd tried to sleep with me). I became friends with a small number of males who were lovely and warned me which people to stay well away from. However, they were not with me all the time, so they could not be there when men tried to touch me as I simply walked back to my cabin alone. Management didn't care because they were doing it, too, only they bribed you with working fewer hours if you went back to their cabins with them. Honestly, it was sick, and staff are really not protected from those vile creatures. Men didn't get away scot-free, either. I regularly saw management bullying the younger boys, shoving them around and threatening them so they'd work faster and harder, even though the boys were doing a fantastic job and working so hard to send money home to their families. I did report the sexual harassment, bullying and illegal working hours to HR, but nothing was looked into, and nobody was spoken to. Management made us clock in for eight hours of work, then made us clock out but continue working, so on paper, it looked as if we were working eight hours and taking breaks, which we weren't.

From the other women, I learnt very quickly that the only way the guys would stop harassing you was when you had an onboard boyfriend. The moment I got with Axel, the harassment stopped. It was so nice, although it was not a great basis for a relationship. I definitely rushed into it, seeking protection more than anything else.

Axel and I spent every day together at work and every evening in my cabin. We got so close so quickly, and he made me feel safe. He showed me off to his friends and practically worshipped me. It felt so good being included in his life, and his friends onboard were so lovely to me. Men told him he was lucky to have me, women told me he was lovely and would treat me well, and people nicknamed us the king and queen.

Axel invited me to his home in the Dominican Republic over Christmas after our contract on the ship had finished. I was so excited: Caribbean Christmas with a sexy man who treated me well—why wouldn't I be excited?

It turned out to be the worst trip ever. I was pushed around and left locked inside the apartment by myself for 17 hours while he went out. Axel stole my money, and his ex-girlfriend smashed his car windows in protest of my being there. Those are just the highlights of my six-week trip in the Dominican.

From day one of my arrival, his ex-girlfriend, the mother of his kids, texted him, saying he'd made a mistake choosing me. This spun me because he'd told me on the ship that they weren't together as things had been difficult, and she didn't want to be with him. It was NOT how I wanted my holiday to start!

Although he would never have admitted it, I believe that when he went home, he led her to think they would get back together because on Christmas Day, she took a bat to his car as she thought I was in his brother's house with Axel and the kids (nah, mate—I was in the apartment drinking warm American wine and watching Spanish TV, neither of which were particularly enjoyable!). Axel told me she kept shouting, asking why wasn't she there with them instead of me. This makes me think he made her believe it could have been an option. Otherwise, why would she have expected to be there instead of me? They weren't together... allegedly.

While she was texting him every day, it brought back memories of B and his ex, and I felt all those familiar feelings; déjà vu, if you like. That really pissed me off because he shouldn't have invited me over if he wasn't completely broken up with his ex. It was not just us women he was messing with; it was his kids, too, as they were caught in the middle of all this.

Axel's whole personality was different when we were on his home turf; he was very controlling and cold. He would just leave the apartment without telling me and come back a few hours later and tell me he didn't have to explain where he'd been to me. Sometimes, he raised his index finger at me and said, 'I'm not talking about this.' He was horrible. It's not like I could go out and visit anyone while he was out, and we were in the middle of nowhere with nothing to see or do.

On reflection, for weeks prior to booking my ticket, my intuition had screamed not to go, but again, I ignored it. My ego told me that Christmas in the Caribbean sunshine with Axel would be better than a cold Christmas at home, but who cares about the sun when you're locked up in an apartment with no phone or internet to talk to anyone, and you're being spoken down to and disrespected on a daily basis? He hadn't treated me that way on the ship, but my gut still told me not to go over. I even started having bad dreams about being there with him. When I was at the airport, waiting to fly over, I felt like crying, but I didn't know why. I know why now, though—it was because, intuitively, I knew it was the wrong thing to do, and I had, yet again, betrayed myself by going full steam ahead regardless. My head said it would be fun, but my emotions were sadness and fear; I really shouldn't have gone.

Axel treated me exactly how I had treated myself: he dismissed my feelings, and so did I. He didn't listen to my needs, and neither did I. He didn't allow me to be my true self, and neither did I. He betrayed me, and so did I. He took from me to give to himself, and I took from me to give to him. I changed so much in the six weeks I was there with him. I really did have to dull down my personality and go along with everything he said or did just to make it through the days. I was numb and had no identity other than the one he assigned to me: to be his provider, financially and sexually.

When I left the Dominican Republic, we both agreed it wasn't going to go any further, and we didn't speak until four years later when he reached out to me on social media after he'd liked some nice photos I'd put up. He asked me how I was, and I ignored it, so he sent me his phone number and said to call him.

What? Was he serious?

I told him I was fine, but I really didn't feel the need to talk any further and asked him to please leave me alone. I then removed him from all my social media accounts and immediately felt as if I had released a heavy weight. Never before had I realised the power in removing someone from your contacts. It seems to remove them from your energy field, too.

That feeling is you telling the universe you no longer wish to hold onto something, and you're letting it go. Some people might say that Axel reached out to me as some form of test from the universe, but I don't believe that. I believe the situations we manifest are reflections of our feelings towards ourselves. For him to contact me was his free will, and perhaps some self-reflection he was going through, but I nipped it in the bud very quickly and prevented any further contact as I valued myself so much more by that time, so I point-blank refused to entertain anything he had to say. I validated myself enough not to need to listen to whatever validation he might have given me. His opinion was no longer important to me.

Self-love is an insanely powerful tool, and it is so influential in how we navigate through our lives. Without self-love, it's tough to navigate. You'll be powerless and unaware, and you'll end up being influenced and navigated by other people, most of whom won't have your best interests at heart. If I'd had that level of self-love when I first met him, I never would have started dating him. That's a key point to think about before starting a relationship. We should ask ourselves how we feel about ourselves, how we feel about the person we are with, what we can give ourselves, and what the other person can give us. If you believe they can provide you with more than you can do for yourself, then tread carefully—you don't want to base your relationship on relying on them to make you feel better. You're already betraying yourself and giving your power and value over to someone else. Unless this partner is able to support you in being your authentic self, without judgement, you really should be careful not to lose yourself in that relationship and allow them to decide your identity based on their perception of you.

CHAPTER 19

Pathways to Profit

I returned home in 2017, feeling as if I were at rock bottom. My travelling days were complete. I had no money, and I had to live with my mum. It was at that point that I moved on from *The Secret* and sought alternative guidance. My thoughts clearly had not manifested the way I wanted them to, so I needed something deeper. My friend, Holly, was a life coach and kundalini yoga teacher, so I began attending her classes. She also introduced me to transcendental meditation (TM). It sounded really odd to me, but I trusted her judgement, and what did I really have to lose? I contacted a TM teacher and went to her house for my first session. It felt so weird, but honestly, what a transformation! TM was so powerful, and it was a huge turning point for me!

TM is practised for 20 minutes twice a day. The technique allows your mind to settle inward, and unlike other forms of meditation, it doesn't involve concentrating on anything or attempting to empty your mind. Trying to empty my mind frustrated me because as I focused on emptying my mind, I got angry at myself for thinking too much. With TM, however, you are given a word by the TM teacher to say to yourself. You use this word until your mind slips gently inward, and you transcend. If you find yourself thinking of something, you simply go back to the word you were given and allow yourself to be guided back inward. Scientific research has proven that TM can help reduce stress and anxiety, provide more energy and increase brain function. I can honestly say that after consistent daily TM practice, I saw huge improvements.

Since returning from the cruise ship in July 2016, I worked as a cleaner for cash-in-hand. I had shit friends and barely any money. When I started TM in April 2017, I was in the same position and not enjoying life. By August 2017, I'd applied for and been successful in gaining a place in an environmental health MSc course, moved to Bristol and got a full-time job. Alongside this, I had reduced my anxiety around driving enough that I was able to drive on the motorway and around Bristol. Gone were the days when I wouldn't go outside my hometown. I'd also gone from looking into getting a teaching degree so I could move to Australia to allowing myself to be guided to the MSc course. When I was researching and applying for teaching courses, I never felt it was something I was fully invested in, but I thought it was a sacrifice I needed to make in order to live in Australia. Even with that, searching for jobs and places to live in Australia didn't fill me with joy. Again, I listened to my thoughts, which told me I could only be happy in Australia, and I had to get a job I didn't actually want to do in order to get there and be happy in the sunshine. Once I started TM and reduced my anxiety and mental 'chatter', I was able to better surrender to the flow of life without judging and/or analysing and/or worrying, and I was quickly and easily guided to the right path for me.

I made friends with really decent people at university and did so well in all my coursework and exams and graduated with distinction. It was incredible for someone who had poor GCSE results and a father who'd told them they'd never be able to get a degree because they were 'Shit at maths and science.'

The reason I was so successful with friendships and my MSc course was that I was on the right path, and TM had allowed me to find that path. Things can't help but go well when you're on the right path. Doors fling open for you, and opportunities fly towards you. The journey feels good. When you find yourself consistently being blocked from going further and continue to have negative experiences, that's a sign that you shouldn't be on your current route; GET OFF!

That's what I found when trying to get into a teaching course to go to Australia. It just didn't make me feel good, and I encountered nothing but blocks and negativity.

In 2018, I was offered a job in Herefordshire. I had never heard of it before, and it really didn't sound like somewhere I wanted to go as it was rural and quiet. I'd spent the last nine years going from Bristol, travelling the world and back to Bristol again. I was used to a busy environment, but I accepted the job because they'd created the position for me as they were so impressed by my interview. As I hadn't yet completed my dissertation for uni, I wasn't eligible for the environmental health officer role, so they went higher up the chain of command and requested that a position be made for me as a technical officer. In addition to that, they offered to pay for my professional training with the Chartered Institute of Environmental Health after I graduated. If that wasn't a sign that I should have accepted the job and moved to Herefordshire, then I don't know what is.

Again, the transition from uni and Bristol to the job and Herefordshire was so smooth and positive. It wouldn't have been so if it was the wrong path.

My starting salary was £23,000. A year later, it was £25,500. So, before taking up TM and kundalini yoga, I had gone from a cleaning job, where I was making approx £800 a year (2016/2017), to £14,000 (2017/2018), £23,000 (2018/2019) and to £25,000 (2019/2020) as a newly qualified environmental health officer. It's just wild how quickly and smoothly everything flowed to me, and it was all because the TM and yoga reduced my anxiety so much that I no longer felt the need to control my life out of fear-based thoughts, and I surrendered to the flow of life. I allowed my emotions to be my guide, and they led me there. None of this was created by my thoughts, as my thoughts were all based around being back in Australia, working in a job I didn't want to do.

Once I began to see results from my consistent TM practices and yoga classes, I naïvely believed my life had been transformed, and I no longer needed to do them anymore. I did not do any inner work at all, and just like a beautiful garden, if not maintained, the garden will be overgrown with weeds. Our minds are like a garden. The weeds that grew over my mind rose up from my subconscious (where they had always been growing) and saturated me with my old, familiar beliefs of not deserving good things and being a shit person. These beliefs also led me to allow another emotionally abusive, toxic person into my life, and in 2019, I met Daniel.

CHAPTER 20

The Termination

I thought things were fine between Daniel and me when we started seeing each other until I fell pregnant. Daniel and I had been using condoms as I wasn't on contraception. When I was a few days late for my period, I wasn't worried because I knew we'd been careful. A week and a half later, I took a test, and it was positive! I didn't panic, but I also knew I wasn't ready for a baby. At that time, I was a lodger in someone's house, and I was on a fixed-term contract at work, so I only had two more years of guaranteed work. If I had a baby at that time, I'd have to move back to my mum's.

Daniel was due to stay at mine on the night I took the test, so I waited until he arrived to tell him in person. He didn't say a lot other than to get rid of it. He then didn't talk any more about it until the following afternoon, when he told me to get rid of it again.

The following evening, he called me to say he'd had a chat with his friends, and they said I was trying to trap him.

What the fuck?

I lost it. I was so angry. 'Trap what, exactly? How fucking dare you? You live in a house share with three grown-ass men in a shit part of Bristol. You drive a 15-year-old car and have a dead-end, minimum-wage job—what the fuck am I trying to trap, exactly?'

He thought that was funny, and he began laughing, so I hung up the phone. I was fuming.

The guy was so influenced by what his friends said that there was no way of making him see the truth. Also, his arrogance at how superior he believed he was to me had had an effect.

The next morning was a Monday, and I went straight to the sexual health clinic, where another test confirmed I was pregnant, and a termination was booked. The nurse advised me that I was six weeks pregnant, which I didn't understand because I hadn't seen Daniel at all six weeks ago. She then explained to me that pregnancy is calculated from the first day of your last period. When I told Daniel this, he used it as a tool to beat and shame me, accusing me of sleeping with someone else and pretending the baby was his to trap him (as if, mate).

I kept repeating that he was the only person I had slept with, and we had been using condoms, so it was an accident. It was at that point he told me that one night, he had taken the condom off. And full disclosure—this is where I have to take accountability for my part that night—I don't remember having sex with him because I was so drunk. I woke up the next morning naked, but I didn't recall having sex the night before. That was why I hadn't realised he had taken off the condom. The next mistake I made was that I didn't admit to him that I couldn't remember because I was ashamed and thought he'd judge me for it, so I kept quiet, and that enabled him to continue accusing me of trapping him. He then tried to manipulate the situation by saying he hadn't felt the need to wear a condom because I was probably lying to him about not being on contraception.

'Excuse me, Daniel? So, I've trapped you into getting me pregnant by telling you we must use condoms because I'm not on contraception?' Well, that was a first! What kind of weird reverse psychology would that have been? Moreover, if I was trying to trap him, telling him to use condoms would have been a shit move on my part. Honestly, that guy made me so angry. How dare he?

He wouldn't come to my appointment with me, so my friend came. I didn't realise terminations were done in two stages, so I had to go back a second time. He made another excuse not to come, saying he had to go to the gym.

I have genuinely never felt so alone, scared, vulnerable or ashamed in my entire life as I did at that hospital. The waiting room was filled with couples, all smiling and happy. I went to sit out in the corridor by myself because it was so triggering.

I trembled when I went into the nurse's room. My breathing was rapid, and my heart thumped. Right before the nurse started the procedure, I burst into uncontrollable tears. The nurse held my hand and said, 'We don't have to do this if you don't want to.'

I said, 'I have to. I can't have a baby with that evil prick.'

The nurses were so good and very patient with me. They knew I was doing it alone, as Daniel had chosen to go to the gym instead. As I had driven myself to the hospital, I was advised to take some of the medication when I got home, as it would make me drowsy.

Once at home, my friend came over to stay with me and help me through it. I had to hide in my bedroom out of my landlady's way because I didn't want her to know. She couldn't conceive and IVF had failed, so I couldn't face her knowing I was wasting the life she desperately wanted. I pretended I was ill, and my friend was over to look after me.

Once I'd passed the foetus in the toilet, I was in pain for hours. I spent most of the night on the bedroom floor on all fours, rocking back and forth to alleviate the pain (and this was in combination with all the medication!). Daniel graced me with a phone call that evening to check on how I was. He was lovely now that he knew the baby was gone.

I was so exhausted, physically and emotionally, and I couldn't have a conversation with him. I needed to concentrate on breathing through the pain. Then, he hit me with the most shocking sentence ever: 'We could try again…for another baby.'

What? It was at that point I ended the conversation. I had no time for more of his nonsense. He was such a dick.

The following two weeks were very difficult. Daniel had changed his mind about the termination and told me he didn't believe in them, I shouldn't have done it, and karma would come back to me because of it. I firmly reminded him that karma would come for both of us. He wasn't absolved of his responsibility in this, despite his attempts. He continued with the narrative that I had tried to trap him, and the baby wasn't his, so we continued to argue. Later that day, he uploaded photos of him and his daughter from a previous relationship on social media and some of him and his mates out drinking in the park.

It was a hot bank holiday, so he was out having fun while I was hiding in my bedroom, bleeding and in pain. I couldn't take it anymore. The emotional pain was way worse than the physical, and I needed a break. I needed to just not be there for a bit. I felt so betrayed, worthless, ashamed, abandoned, ignored and dismissed, and I hated myself.

I bought some beer to mix with my codeine medication. I didn't intend to kill myself as such, but as I emptied the pills into my hand, I did think that if I never woke up, it wouldn't be a bad thing. So, I took all the pills, sat on my bed and drank the beer, waiting to be knocked out so I could be free of all the pain.

When I awoke the next morning, my first thought was, 'Fuck's sake, it didn't work.' I've probably got a high tolerance from all the drugs I used to do a few years prior.

I decided to see a counsellor and found the sessions incredibly useful, as they made me aware of how I had been punishing myself. I needed to allow myself to grieve and forgive myself. I was also to allow myself to tell Daniel how

I really felt and not hide it for fear of receiving more verbal abuse and manipulation from him. I was advised to do this by writing a letter to him (but not sending it). That way, I could be totally vulnerable and authentic in a safe environment.

I felt a shift when I finished the letter, and I discovered things I didn't know I was feeling. I blamed myself so much that I'd forgotten what Daniel's role had been in everything. I had spent the whole time defending myself from his accusations and abuse I had unconsciously taken on the responsibility of having caused it all myself. Writing that letter allowed me to recognise and remember that he'd played a huge role, too, so I felt better equipped to tell him how his behaviour had made me feel.

I didn't send him the letter, but I took excerpts from it and put them into text messages.

He replied, 'I love you.'

Obviously, Daniel and I didn't work out. How could we come back from that? I hated him so much. I couldn't be around him and act as if nothing had happened and forget about the way he had treated me at my lowest point.

I also came to realise that guy had chosen to have sex with me without a condom when I was drunk, so drunk that I didn't remember it happening. He'd then accused me of sleeping with someone else, of trapping him and lying about not being on contraception. I don't know what had to happen to someone to make them think that behaviour was okay. I understood that he wanted to deflect his guilt onto me to absolve himself. However, he'd manipulated and verbally abused me, knowing full well he'd also played a part in it, and he refused to take any form of accountability.

Since I've opened up about this, I have heard similar stories from other women. It's crazy how something that takes two people can be blamed on just one. It's also so outdated and lazy to accuse a woman of trapping a man. It's a baby, a human life—it's not a contract.

I realise that termination is a controversial decision to make, and I realise there are single mothers out there who do an incredible job, but it was the right decision for me. I didn't want to be tied to Daniel. I didn't want to move into my mum's with a baby. I didn't have the money for a baby, and despite what Daniel had claimed, he didn't have money either. I had more than he did. In addition to all of this, I also didn't want a baby with someone who'd slept with me without a condom when I was drunk and then blamed me for the pregnancy. That was not a path I wanted to take for my future.

It's easy to say, 'I wouldn't have done that.' I honestly never thought I'd be in that position, and yet I was, and I had to make the best decision for myself. Since that experience, I've realised that we have no right to judge other people's decisions. Everyone has a reason or a story as to why they do what they do, and we may never know the full extent of it. Also, it's none of our business what someone is or has been going through. I like to believe that most people are just trying their best despite judgement from others. Because I was so scared of Daniel judging me, I never admitted to him that I couldn't remember anything from the night before and that my last memory was being sat on the sofa. If I had known we'd had unprotected sex, I could have taken a morning-after pill, and none of this would have happened. Instead, I kept quiet then received judgement from him when I fell pregnant. I felt I would be judged for being so wasted and not remembering having sex, and yet I didn't judge him for sleeping with me when I was in that condition.

I'd attacked and betrayed myself from the get-go, and that, in turn, allowed Daniel the opportunity to attack and betray me, too. I've never held him accountable for his actions, and he, in turn, didn't hold himself accountable either. It was an incredibly painful lesson, but if I'd felt safe to speak my truth, it would have saved us all from pain. If I'd had more self-esteem, I would have felt safe to have spoken out. It was at that point that I had to change everything I thought I knew.

CHAPTER 21

Fresh Choices, Fresh Paths

I literally stopped everything related to my love life. I blocked the phone numbers of guys I'd had a thing with in the past. I stopped drinking in the same bars. I stopped hanging around with certain people. I stopped myself from going anywhere near men. I'd had a wake-up call, and I needed to pay attention to what I was doing and take accountability. My life needed to change. I had now clocked three occasions where I would have preferred to die than be in the relationship: as a child, when I was being sexually abused, while suffering from depression, living with my boyfriend, and now this with Daniel and the termination. When you experience low points like these, it's time to make different choices. So, I began implementing them and started doing yoga, meditation, and exercising much more regularly. I joined yoga and gym classes so I could surround myself with new people.

My car broke down one day, so my yoga teacher arranged for a girl in our class to pick me up. This girl, Kelly, became a good friend of mine and the wonderful teacher I really needed at that point. Kelly introduced me to cacao ceremonies and soul retrievals. I genuinely believe my car was supposed to break down so my friendship with Kelly could be orchestrated. During that time, I began practicing EFT (Emotional Freedom Technique) consistently. My friend Holly, who had previously introduced me to TM, demonstrated how to do EFT and lent me a book from Nick Ortner, the CEO of 'The Tapping Solution'. Nick has written books and created an app, along with his siblings, demonstrating to people how to use EFT for a range of issues. Keen to make a positive change to my life, I went back to the book and began implementing a daily practice.

Nick Ortner describes EFT, on his website, thetappingsolution.com,[6] as the process of tapping on specific meridian points whilst talking through traumatic or negative memories. Meridian points are mapped throughout the body, and energy circulates through your body along this network of channels. Our bodies are made up of energy, and when this energy is disrupted, we feel negative emotions. Tapping restores balance to the body's energy, and the emotional and physical symptoms are reduced or resolved. The technique starts with focusing on a bad memory or fear whilst tapping on each of the meridian points, which sends signals to the amygdala. This is the primal part of our brains, where we get our fight, flight or freeze responses. Fight is where we feel

---

[6] Ortner, N. (n.d.) *The Tapping Solution*. https://www.thetappingsolution.com/

triggered to fight the perceived threat, perhaps a person. Flight is where we run away from the threat, and freeze is where our body cannot move and we are frozen in that situation, unable to escape. When you experience trauma, the amygdala is triggered and releases excessive amounts of cortisol, known as the 'stress hormone'. Tapping can help to reduce or eliminate the stress response by sending new signals to your mid-brain.

EFT is so good that I even use it for hay fever relief now. I have suffered from hay fever since I was a child and have always relied upon tablets and eyedrops to get rid of the symptoms. It is said that itchy eyes and a runny nose are biological responses to the pollen, triggered once the pollen is inhaled into the body. Once this response is activated, and your body starts to fight the perceived threat, the itchy eyes and runny nose occur, which, in turn, cause distress to the individual, further exacerbating the symptoms. Once I discovered that you could do EFT tapping to relieve yourself of this, I decided to give it a try. What was the worst that could happen? It wouldn't work, and I'd have to continue with my tablets and eye drops, right? After a walk in a park that had recently been mowed, my eyes became itchy, and my nose ran. I found a lady on YouTube who demonstrated how to calm the biological responses using EFT, and I followed her directions. It took a few minutes to integrate, but once it did, my body relaxed, and my eyes and nose settled back down to their normal states. I haven't bought tablets or eye drops for years now, as I do EFT when the symptoms kick in. I am in no way cured of hay fever—I have just been given a tool to use that relieves me of it when my body reacts badly to any pollen I might have inhaled.

Whilst exploring these new practices, my inner self began to change, resulting in the transformation of my outer world. I moved into a new home with two great housemates, my physical body was fitter, my friendships were happier, and I was doing a lot of multi-agency work with the police and fire services. I was surrounded by professional men who treated me with a lot of respect without wanting sex in return, which was a first for me. They valued what I had to say, they encouraged me to voice my opinions and they praised me for being me without trying to sleep with me. These were men who also talked about their wives and girlfriends with respect. It was an incredible exposure for me because I had never been in an environment where smart, decent, successful men liked and respected me for my personality and not because it was part of a plan to get me into bed. Some of these men talked to me about their families with great respect, and it just blew me away to discover that men like this existed. I couldn't ever imagine my dad doing the same when it came to myself and my brothers or being respectful about my mum. I remember when someone set fire to a recycling bin in the village where I grew up, and my dad's response to hearing about it was, 'It was probably one of my kids.' It was NONE of us kids.

He also had a habit of slagging us kids off to his parents, and my nan would come back to me full of judgements that weren't based on any truths. So, with that being my example of a supportive father, I was amazed to witness grown men talking so nicely about their families. It was really lovely. This exposure made me realise there were different calibres of men out there that I respected and admired. I just hadn't met them before because I had allowed myself to remain a prisoner to my past experiences and beliefs, and therefore, I continued to attract the same kind of toxic men.

The longer I spent with this new crowd of people, the more my self-esteem grew. I was no longer suppressed and manipulated. I was not criticised when I gave an opinion. I was heard and allowed to speak freely. This also had an impact on my job performance, and subsequently, I was given more responsibility. I really began to excel at and loved my job! I discovered parts of my personality I didn't know I had and began to do things I didn't know I was capable of, all because I had put myself in an environment where I was allowed to be me without criticism, control, or judgement.

I discovered I had a desire to be in a career where I could bring justice to victims and hold people accountable for their actions. I realised I wanted to give a voice to the voiceless and power to the powerless. Anything involving an injustice triggered me, and I realised that I should put it to good use and help others for a living.

In 2022, I landed a job working for an organisation as an investigator. It was a huge shift in direction from anything I ever thought I would be involved in. The confidence and ability I discovered in myself was gained when I made the change to cut out certain people and places of my life and surrounding myself with different people in new environments. I was encouraged to make these changes by following my feelings and changing my mind-set.

Reflecting on my career, I realised I had attracted temporary jobs rather than permanent ones. This was because I hadn't felt settled since returning from travelling. My head and my heart were in various countries around the world (particularly Australia), and I never felt truly grounded or settled back in England. I was never fully present there.

At the end of 2021, I felt an overwhelming urge for security and felt ready to put down roots by getting a permanent job and buying my own home. When the job advertisement for the investigating officer role for the organisation came up, I felt confident enough to do it. I applied and got the job! Having secured that permanent role, I was confident I could buy my own home shortly after. I visualised having a two-bedroom property with a garden (which seemed a little out of my league, given the increase in house prices and mortgage rates). However, I stopped listening to other people's opinions and negativity. I didn't allow myself to focus on those perceived 'blocks' to get my home; I just visualised and desired my two-bedroom home, searching the internet for interior design ideas and imagining myself living there. My feelings and thoughts were in perfect alignment with each other, which meant I had laser focus on my goal, and therefore, manifested it with minimal effort.

I began receiving more money on top of my regular monthly wage by taking on another role as an expert witness, using my environmental health knowledge. I didn't have to work many hours, but I received a lot of money in return. Very quickly, I reached my goal of £13,000 to put down a 10% deposit on a property, and then I had more money on top of that. I first began saving back in 2019, but it was going very slowly as I was trapped in the belief that I wouldn't be able to afford a decent place, and I still didn't feel secure enough to know that buying a home was the right idea for me. Once it become clear, at the end of 2021, that buying a home was what I desired and I was ready for a permanent job, I released any limiting beliefs around it and remained laser-focused on the end goal. Every day, I imagined and felt myself in that permanent job, living in my two-bedroom home. I didn't plan or work out how I would achieve my goals; I just allowed them to unfold, knowing they would happen for me. With that, my job and my home were both offered to me within three weeks of each other.

Regarding the job and the home, I once had ideas they would both be in Bristol. Allowing that requirement to dissolve opened me up to more opportunities. The investigating job I had allowed me to work all over the UK, which I loved, and the home was in a beautiful part of Herefordshire, close to all amenities and surrounded by lovely neighbours. Everything I desired and put my thoughts and feelings into alignment with appeared effortlessly in my reality. I enjoyed the journey getting there, which made it easy. If I had refused to release the idea of living in Bristol, I'd still be living at mum's now, saving money, waiting for what I wanted to materialise but didn't exist for me. If it was meant to happen, it would have, and I wouldn't have been nudged to look in Herefordshire, where it all happened so quickly and easily. I even knocked down the asking price by £5,000, leaving me with extra money to buy a new kitchen as soon as I moved in.

My home was perfect, and I loved it so much. Every room was refurbished, and it was incredible to see the designs created in my head materialise in real life.

In the book A Course in Miracles, Marianne Williamson says there is no such thing as sacrifice. If I had held onto the belief that I was going to buy the home I wanted in Bristol, I would have had to sacrifice on space, comfort, convenience and finances. We are meant to be 'attractors' and not 'pursuers'. I had pursued a place in Bristol until I gave it up and attracted my beautiful home in Herefordshire. When visualising the home I wanted, I enjoyed looking online and creating a vision board of how I wanted it to look. I was enjoying the process and therefore, softened any resistance to it, allowing it to flow to me easily.

I had gained wonderful new experiences and achieved goals others thought wouldn't be possible (particularly buying a home in the middle of a cost-of-living crisis and paying for the bills, mortgage and refurbishment all by myself). I had managed to make life work for me and was completely bossing it. At my core, however, my beliefs about unsafe and toxic relationships were still present. This is what caused me to unconsciously attract another lesson.

CHAPTER 22

Tears on the Chicago Skyline

I met Tyler in April 2022, within weeks of being offered my new job and finding my home. He seemed decent on the surface. He had a good job as a soldier, he behaved like a gentleman, and he was always keen to get out and do things together. It was really refreshing and just what I wanted. He even gave me his car to use so I didn't have to buy a new one after mine had broken down again. That was great! However, I had a nagging feeling that he was hiding something.

He seemed to be leading a double life that he didn't include me. He would go away on weekends to see his son in Reading or work security at festivals throughout the summer and while he was doing this, he never made any contact with me. Sometimes, he was gone from Friday to Monday, and I wouldn't hear from him until Tuesday, which was fine if we'd both decided it was just an occasional hook-up, but we hadn't decided that. Monday—or sometimes Tuesday—to Thursday, Tyler love-bombed the hell out of me, always wanting to talk to me and see me. I was the best thing since sliced bread during the week and a nobody on the weekend. When I raised this with him, he said it was because he was busy, or I was just being insecure. I actually don't think checking in with someone you're seeing is a lot to ask for unless you're not that interested, and if you're not interested, don't act as if you are when it suits.

As he'd lent me his car and invited me to his friend's wedding in Chicago, I felt compelled to stay with him despite my feelings that he was leading a double life. By staying with him, I essentially allowed him to continue leading his double life with no explanation or apology. This also allowed him to dismiss me whenever I wanted to question where I stood with him. Tyler had a dismissive-avoidant attachment style, which means he didn't know how to deal with or regulate emotions, so he would dismiss or avoid anything close to emotional. Whenever he was going through tough times with his ex, their kid or work, I always listened to him and helped him in any way I could. When I had a concern about something, he didn't want to talk about it, and he dismissed me and cut off the conversation quickly. This was another example of how treating people the way you want to be treated just doesn't work. After all these years, I was beginning to allow myself to feel how I truly felt and act upon my feelings rather than suppress myself, so I found being with Tyler very tough because I couldn't be my true self around him. After four months, I literally couldn't take it anymore and ended it with him. I just couldn't bear him and how small and disrespected I felt by him. I had felt that way with other guys, too, but I felt it stronger with Tyler because I was listening to myself and my needs more than I had ever done before. I had given up caring about the car and the trip to Chicago, and I just wanted out.

A week after finishing with Tyler, he called me, owning up to taking me for granted, apologising for excluding me from the other side of his life and promising to be better if I gave him another chance. He told me he loved me, but I didn't say it back because I knew I didn't love him. I'll only say it if I mean it, not when I want to manipulate someone into yielding to my needs. I began to feel sorry for him, and as we already had Chicago planned, I told him we'd take it slow, go to Chicago in a few weeks and see how we were then. It was a really dumb reason for giving him another chance when I knew I was going to be unhappy again. I essentially sacrificed my peace of mind in exchange for a trip to Chicago. I'd put the trip to Chicago first over my feelings, when really, I didn't need Tyler to take me to Chicago—I could have taken myself there. I've travelled the world, and most of it by myself, but I just got caught up in believing I needed him to get something I wanted.

Looking back, when I booked the flights, I had this nervous feeling, like the one I'd had when booking my flights to the Dominican Republic to see Axel. I just felt so uneasy, and I kept putting it off. I eventually booked the flights after Tyler told me they had to be done by the end of the day as his friend needed to know when we were arriving. I should have been honest with myself, acted upon how I felt and told him I wouldn't be going, but I didn't.

I hated the holiday before we'd even left England. He annoyed me the whole drive to Heathrow. After having a few weeks away from him when I'd ended it, I had forgotten just how immature he was. I felt suffocated, and I could see much more clearly how manipulative and shady he was.

Once we got to Chicago, he didn't introduce me to any of his friends. I had to walk up to them and introduce myself, which was awkward.

Three days into the holiday, I found out he'd slept with another girl behind my back some months prior. She told me she didn't know he was with me at the time. I was fuming, especially because, when I confronted him, he didn't say a word: nothing, *nada*, *rien*. The other girl said that she was sorry, and she explained everything to me, but he stayed silent. Over 24 hours after hearing this news, he was still giving me the silent treatment, so I lost my temper and shouted at him. The reason I waited so long to get angry was because I was partially relieved that he had been messing around behind my back, because now I had proof that my instinct was right, and I had a great reason to get rid of him for good. But after being ignored for more than a whole day, I felt really disrespected that he wouldn't offer me an explanation and take accountability like the other girl had, and this angered me. Once I'd shouted at him, his response was to call a taxi. He left our hotel on Monday at 11.00 a.m., and I didn't see him again until 4.00 a.m. Tuesday.

During that time, I had no idea where he was, and I didn't know where his friends lived, nor did I have any of their numbers to call. I spent the entire day alone, feeling hurt, disrespected, rejected and in shock. In the evening, I drank two bottles of wine in the hotel, and my anger grew. I texted, asking where he was, but he ignored me. Even a simple, 'I'm in town with my mates. I don't feel like talking right now. Not sure when I'll be back' would have been sufficient for me, but he wouldn't allow me that. I had to be punished for daring to confront him and demanding an explanation.

It was now nearing 48 hours since I had been given the news, and I was still receiving nothing but silence from him. I was raging!

While sitting in the bath, drinking wine, I emptied the contents of his suitcase in the bath with me and sent him a photo. I made sure he could clearly see his leather jacket and shoes along with his groomsman suit he had only bought a few weeks ago. I knew it had cost him a lot of money because he kept complaining about how expensive it was and how he couldn't afford it, so I made sure it got a good soaking. Tyler was always broke, just like all the other men I had been with. I had paid for the hotel and knew he wouldn't pay me back, so I didn't care about damaging his clothes. Fuck him. A few weeks ago, he'd loved me, and now he was punishing me and disrespecting me.

Once the bath started getting cold, I got out and felt like doing more damage, so I drained the water out and poured red wine on his white clothes (especially the expensive groomsman shirt) and sent him a photo. I then popped the lenses out of his Ray-Bans, smashed his watch and stole the $10 he had in his suitcase.

I called Rachel in Australia, and we talked for ages. She was so helpful in calming me back down, and it was comforting to speak to someone as I'd been in Chicago four days and spent most of it alone.

Once we'd ended our conversation, I was calm enough to fall asleep, but was woken at 4.00 a.m. by Tyler at the door. I opened it, and he was standing there with a takeaway pizza box in his hand. My first thought was that the dickhead had been out on the piss all night in town, ignoring me, not giving a shit how I was, and I was mad!

I snatched the pizza from his hand and slammed the door shut in his face. I was about to tuck into the pizza but then decided I wasn't finished with him yet, so I went back to open the door and found him lying on the floor. I grabbed his coat, pulled him up and punched him in the side of the face. He ran off across the car park, so I chased after him in my nightdress, barefoot, but I lost him when he ran through some trees and hedges. It was dark and cold and I didn't have anything on my feet, so I calmly went back to my room, locked the door, and began tucking into that pizza.

The next morning, I was still angry, so I went over to his clothes that were still in the bathtub and peed all over them—twice, actually. Those urine-soaked clothes remained like that over the next two days because he didn't come back to collect them. I imagine he borrowed his friend's clothes.

I then took a taxi into town and went sightseeing, enjoying as much of the day as I could because I had arranged to fly home the following day, which was a day earlier than we had planned. On the day I checked out of the hotel, the receptionist let me off the early check-out fee as she knew everything that had been going on between Tyler and me. She was so lovely, and she really wanted to make sure I was okay. She knew I had paid for the hotel, so she said she wouldn't allow him to come back and use the room for the remaining night I had already paid for. She asked me to bring his suitcase to reception and tell him he needed to come and collect it from her.

I dragged the damp, urine-soaked clothes in the suitcase—I hadn't taken into account just how heavy the case would be. Oh, my word! It went from 23 kg to (I guess) 63 kg! The thing was heavy! I had to use both hands to pull it to reception. I couldn't even lift it up the small step into reception. I also left a trail of water from the room down to reception, and whenever I stopped walking, a pool of water collected on the floor. People looked at me open-mouthed as they witnessed the trail of water behind me, but I held my head high and continued on.

I had to leave the case outside to dry off.

I texted him to tell him to collect his things, then jumped into a taxi and headed for the airport.

I had been so angry the past few days that I hadn't had the capacity to cry. Once at the airport, everything began sinking in properly, and I could finally cry, so much so that strangers came up to me to check if I was okay. All Tyler had to do was acknowledge and offer some form of explanation for that girl's story, and things would have ended much differently. I didn't want to be with him; of that I was definitely sure, but I still feel like I was owed a conversation, at least. After all, they had slept together at a time when I wanted to be with him, so I still felt the betrayal.

On the plane home, I was adamant to myself that I must change and resolve whatever crap it was that I was subconsciously holding on to ensure I stopped attracting the same characters and situations. I'd reached my mid-thirties—that shit should NOT be happening anymore! By the time you reach your mid-thirties, your personality is complete, and I knew that from then on, I would continue repeating those patterns unless I had an intervention.

Tyler was an example of someone who repeated patterns—six months after I had last seen him in Chicago, he got married. It wasn't to the girl he had cheated on me with but to another girl I had never heard of before. That was his second marriage, and that one was also quick—he'd met, married and separated from his first wife in less than 12 months. Two years later, he was getting married again only months after we'd split up. The guy was terrified of being alone and was deeply insecure.

There were two good endings to this story. Firstly, I no longer have him in my life, so I am free from his manipulation. Secondly, he had to leave his entire suitcase in Chicago because it was drenched in Shiraz and urine, so he couldn't take it on the plane, and he returned home wearing the same clothes he'd been wearing the night I'd lost him in the bushes.

CHAPTER 23

And Now, The Healing Can Begin

My new job and new home were helpful distractions from what had happened with Tyler. Not having him in my life anymore made me feel relieved. The anxious, distrusting feeling I constantly had whilst with him had dissolved, and I felt light and free. I thought then that I had healed and no further action was required, but unfortunately, it doesn't work like that. To make completely sure I ended my toxic pattern, I had to address my suppressed issues. As much as I wanted to ignore and run away from them, I had to pull the weeds from the roots and confront the sexual abuse I'd encountered as a child. I just had to do it. All of my patterns of betrayal and abandonment have been learnt from this experience. My life had to come back around full circle if I were to break this trauma bond once and for all.

I started following guidance from Eckhart Tolle, in his book *The Power of Now*, and discovered that people treated me the way I treated myself. For example, I consistently abandoned my needs to put someone else's first, and this resulted in people doing the same to me. Once I'd integrated this lesson, all my past situations became crystal clear, and I released for me. I now realise the part I played in the circumstances that happened for myself. I say 'for' me and not 'to' me because the external experiences were a manifestation of my internal beliefs. I just needed to treat myself the way I wanted others to treat me.

Abraham Hicks[7] says you should give yourself the things you want and keep yourself in a high vibrational state. I thought I was doing this, but unconsciously, I still expected happiness to come from external influences. I had been ignoring and suppressing my gut feelings, which resulted in my receiving people who also ignored and suppressed my feelings. I had to learn to practice compassionate self-talk. When you respond to painful emotions with negative self-talk, you are, in fact, training your brain to feel shame over feeling bad. I had spent my entire life belittling and criticising myself. In order to grow and lead a more fulfilling life, I had to change how I treated myself and just forget about anyone else. I also realised I had to start setting and enforcing healthy boundaries. You can't be emotionally healthy if you never stand up for yourself and your own needs and wants.

I spent the next year in full healing mode. I did EFT, reiki, TM, and kundalini yoga, and I read *The Power of Now* and *A Course in Miracles*. After a few months of consistent, daily practice, it all started to integrate, and I genuinely never

---

[7] Hicks & Hicks, 2009

felt that level of peace ever before in my entire life. All these tools highlighted where I was still subconsciously holding on to pain and trauma, things I wasn't aware I was still carrying around. I had a fear of being seen and heard. This didn't make sense initially because I have lots of friends, and I've travelled the world and met many people, but I pushed myself to do things despite the fear of it. The EFT helped me discover this fear stemmed from the sexual abuse because I didn't feel safe to be seen. I didn't want him to see me. I wanted to fade into the background and not be seen. I began to understand why I didn't feel safe to be my authentic self.

In addition to the sexual abuse, I learnt that I had both the mother and father wounds. It is said that an adult who has mother wounds demonstrates the following symptoms:

- body shame
- lack of boundaries
- desire to fix or rescue others
- feels threatened by other women
- uncomfortable to speak their truth because of shame or fear

The symptoms of father wounds include:

- low self-esteem and confidence
- feels as if they are not good enough
- oppresses, shames, or abuses others

- fearful or distrusting of men
- attracts emotionally unavailable partners

These are the most common symptoms of mother and father wounds, and I had all of these. To be honest, most people around the planet do! I am not unique in this way. The difference is that I'm talking about it, and talking about it is the starting point to overcoming it. I used to hate hearing people complain that their lives were bad because their mum or dad didn't treat them a certain way, and I'd think they were making excuses for their poor behaviour. Although I still think this to a certain extent, I also have some compassion now that I understand how the body and mind store trauma, which makes us act in ways that keep us safe. The brain is mostly predictive, guessing the next thing coming our way as it tries to keep us alive and safe. Our predictions are based on our past experiences. For some, acting out of aggression or being on the defensive may be from past memories being triggered and the stress responses that come with them. Most people are unaware that the subconscious runs the show and don't, therefore, realise how they are behaving, blaming other people for their problems and further disempowering themselves. Releasing others from our blame is incredibly freeing and transformative.

I could pick out situations where my parents made me feel all the symptoms of mother and father wounds, but it really wouldn't do any good analysing and putting a story to it. That would just invoke more energy for the problem, and where energy goes, energy flows. I don't want to create more of the same—I want to release! This is where the book *The Power of Now* is transformative. It taught me the power of presence, staying present on the feeling (not the story), and just allowing it to be there until it is released and transmuted. Then, when it comes back in a day, a week, a month, or a year, simply follow the same process and release and transmute it again.

For anybody who thinks it can't be that easy and it won't work, just try it. There is literally nothing to lose. If nothing else has worked for you so far, then stop flogging a dead horse and try practicing presence. Although I've healed most of my mother and father wounds; I still occasionally feel them come up (i.e., low confidence and not feeling good enough), so I remain present with them until they have been transmuted into more peaceful feelings. Healing is not linear. There will always be people, events and situations where negative emotions are triggered. Healing is not a diet—it's a lifestyle. My problem in the past was that I would do a few months of kundalini yoga and read a book on manifesting and think I was ready to live my best life, but I wasn't living my best life because I wasn't consistent when doing the practices. Doing inner work needs to be incorporated into your daily life for you to be able to see the real benefits. I don't do yoga, TM, reiki or EFT every day—I wouldn't be getting on with the rest of my day if I did! Also, I don't want to do all of them every day. It would overwhelm me, resulting in my stopping all of them and slipping back into my old mindset.

The one thing I do every single day is practice presence. The moment I feel off, I check in with my body, and if I can, there and then, I sit with the emotion, allowing it to be there, watching it, feeling it and waiting for it to move its way up through my body to be released and transmuted. If I can't be present in that particular moment, I simply acknowledge how I feel and let myself know that I will give myself the time and presence I need as soon as I can. Essentially, I am emotionally available to myself, something I have never been to me before and certainly something I have never received from a partner.

I don't blame my parents for the mother and father wounds I've adopted. In fact, I don't even acknowledge those symptoms as mother and father wounds. I mentioned those labels to echo what is being used in the wider world, but I choose not to use those terms because I feel it puts more emphasis on the story behind the symptoms. We don't want to include the story because our brains will continue to focus on it, and it'll disrupt the healing process. You have to feel it to heal it 'cos the brain is pain!

When I look at the upbringing my parents had from their caregivers, I can clearly see how they unconsciously developed—and therefore exhibited—their behaviours. They played this out for my brothers and me growing up so that we would observe, copy and pass on to the next generation. What I'm doing now is known as generational healing. The time I took to heal was the intervention needed to disrupt any copying and passing on of the same generational 'curses'. For example, I can see striking similarities in my mum and her mum: no boundaries, people-pleasing behaviour, afraid to speak up and easily controlled. I also see similarities between my dad and his dad: no respect for boundaries, critical, unsupportive and controlling.

These are behaviours my parents learnt from their parents, which were likely picked up from their parents, too. This is why I hold no blame towards any of them. I realise just how blessed I am to be alive at this point in time when we have access to information that teaches us about these things. Give me a few seconds online, and I'll pull up lots of information on generational healing, behavioural patterns, and trauma bonds (it may not all be accurate, but you will soon learn what resonates and what doesn't). My parents and all those before them didn't have access to this valuable information, so they operated with their subconscious, which was shaped by their childhood experiences. It's okay to be annoyed at our parents, sometimes, for things they might have done that hurt you, but don't allow it to consume you and define who you are.

There is a false allegation about healing, that you are supposed to be this super-happy, peaceful person, with your head in the clouds with unicorns and rainbows, meditating and eating tofu. I can assure you that is not it! Healing is about identifying, pulling up and weeding out the trauma your body has stored throughout your life, transmuting it into more peaceful, positive energy. Just like layers of an onion, you peel a part away, leaving you feeling great. Then, at some point in time, another layer of crap emerges in need of peeling off, which leaves you feeling good again. So, if you're thinking, 'Well, what's the point, then, if I'm gonna bring up bad memories that make me feel like shit?' I urge you to ask how happy you are right now. How well is your life going right now? If you can't truthfully answer ten out of ten immediately (before your brain convinces you otherwise), then you're not operating at your best level. You deserve to feel ten out of ten in every area of your life, so if you're not, simply trying inner work may help you achieve a higher level of peace or happiness. You won't change anything if you're not willing to change something first. The universe will not bring you everything you want if you are not going to put in the work. I'm not peaceful and happy every day, but I certainly no longer cry when I wake up in the morning because I don't want to be alive. I no longer struggle for money. I no longer suppress myself to pacify a partner.

The inner work has helped me peel away the layers of the onion, stripping away those parts that allowed me to exhibit behaviours that attracted negative situations to me. The inner work has helped me level up, and the more benefits I feel in my body and see in my reality, the more I want to continue doing it. As I said before, it is not a diet; it's a lifestyle. Whether you are doing the inner work or not, you will encounter negative experiences. The difference is that when you take the time to heal, those experiences will be few and far between in comparison to those experienced by people who are not doing the inner work. Once you have rewired the neurons firing in your brain, developed different beliefs and calmed your nervous system, you will consciously create a more enriching, fulfilling life.

Self-reflection is incredibly important as it allows us to examine ourselves and make a decision to alter our behaviours to produce better outcomes. The more you observe yourself, the more you awaken from the unconscious mind to the conscious mind. Once you take committed, consistent action to be self-aware, you will create a new mind and way of thinking. Joe Dispenza describes it as stopping the same firing and wiring of old neural networks related to the old personality as you interrupt the feelings associated with those thoughts, and therefore, no longer signal genes in the same way. Further, he suggests that the longer you remain in emotional creation rather than a survival state, your mind and body will be in alignment with your desired outcomes. The nerve cells that once fired together to form your old self are no longer wired together, and your old personality is being 'biologically dismantled'.

Having become aware of my fear of being seen and heard, I worked to create new beliefs around it. I allowed these fears to be felt and transmuted into feelings of being safe to be seen and heard. After a few months of committed practice, I experienced a shift in my outer reality when I attended a work meeting. I hated meetings so much. It was because having a group of people look at me while I talked gave me anxiety to the point where I would make excuses not to attend. I just couldn't stand people looking at me and believing they would mock or judge me for what I had to say. I felt inferior, as if my voice had no place to be heard.

One day, a few months after working on my fear of being seen and heard, I was travelling to a team meeting feeling positive about it and singing in the car on the way. That was the first meeting in my life where I spoke up, asked questions, and gave opinions, feeling completely relaxed the whole time. Everybody listened to me and valued what I had to say. It was a massive breakthrough! I'm not completely absolved of that fear, but I have resolved it to a level where my life has benefited from it and become easier. I now believe that what I have to say has value, and I feel confident speaking up. Equally, I also feel confident not talking too much in circumstances where I previously over-explained out of anxiety or to defend myself. I am comfortable not feeling the need to convince someone to believe me.

CHAPTER 24

The Road to Renewal

During my healing work, I became aware of past events that were distorted in my mind because of other people's influences, and I was finally able to see them for what they were rather than what other people told me they were. A prime example was something that happened back in 2009. My dad picked me up from university after an exam, and I felt shit because it was tough, and I didn't feel it had gone well. In the car, my dad kept messing around, telling bad jokes and interrupting me every few seconds, making fun of me when I was trying to talk about the exam. I got exhausted and said I didn't want to talk anymore. He didn't like that, and he told me I needed to talk.

I refused—I was done.

He began threatening to kick me out the car if I didn't talk but I didn't react to this threat even though I knew he was being serious.. He then dropped me off at the next motorway services. I quietly got out of the car and watched him take my suitcase out of the back. He put it on the floor and said, 'Bye.'

I didn't say a word. I wasn't going to be bullied and intimidated into doing what he wanted. I went into the services and asked around for someone to give me a lift back to Somerset. A man dropped me off at my hometown, and my friend collected me. She already knew what had happened—word had already spread around the pub. It turned out that as soon as my dad had dropped me off, he called my mum to tell her I had been 'gobby' with him, and he had warned me that if I didn't stop, he would kick me out. He then alleged that I'd ignored his warning and continued being 'gobby', so he kicked me out.

What… The… Fuck? As if that's what happened!

When I arrived at the pub, everyone was laughing at me, saying I deserved it, and I should have listened to him, that it was my own fault, and so on. I was so shocked at the story he had chosen to tell. He'd thrown me under the bus, lied about me and humiliated me to make himself sound like the hero of the story when the truth was that he hadn't respected my boundaries when I said I didn't want to talk. He hadn't respected or cared that I was feeling low because of my exam. It had angered him that he couldn't make me do what he wanted. He didn't care that he'd left me at the services, where I could have got into a car with a pervert. Luckily for me, I'm pretty resilient, and it only took me ten minutes to find a staff member heading back to Somerset.

This story has come up over the years, and everyone (apart from Mum and Rachel) all believed Dad's lies about that day. I even had one of his colleagues tell me in the pub that he was at work laughing about it to them all. He's been called a 'legend' for kicking me out of the car when I was 'gobby'. This was my own father telling lies about me, creating a narrative that enabled him to seem superior, knowingly allowing people to laugh at me and blame me for what happened.

Now that I've realised my feelings are valid and I deserve to be heard, I know I've nothing to be ashamed of. I only felt that way because I allowed his story to convince me I should be ashamed. It was made harder because other people believed him. It's tough and exhausting when your voice becomes lost underneath everyone else's, but I don't feel like that anymore. I'm so much more secure now, so I'm happy to give my side without feeling shame. I don't feel bad for exposing the truth of my dad's behaviour because he didn't protect me. Years later, I got him to talk about it in a text, and he admitted that I wasn't being 'gobby,' but my being quiet made him feel uncomfortable. I took a screenshot of the message because I knew he would change his story again when we had an audience. He likes to tell the family that he taught me a lesson, but all he taught me was not to trust him. I proved I wouldn't be bullied and threatened, and that was all.

As I've been doing the inner work and allowing myself to be authentically me, I've watched how my outer world has transformed, too. My flat has been refurbished beautifully. It's so peaceful and cosy, just how I feel internally. I've had the finances to enable me to create this wonderful environment. My social life has been fun, and I love my friends so much! I've upgraded my wardrobe, my vocabulary, the places I socialise, and finally, my men. The upgrade to my men isn't happening quickly, but at least it is happening. With each guy, they get better looking, better in personality, have better jobs and lead better lives. It makes sense this is happening because as I upgrade myself, I upgrade my external life, and I'm just attracting men who are in alignment with me. It didn't start off like that, though. I'd say that, for the first four or five months, I was exposed to photos of people who had hurt me on social media, who were living their best lives and parading their happiness online. This infuriated me, and I felt that familiar feeling of unfairness again. How did they get that, and I didn't? I took the time to be alone and work to create a better version of myself so I could live a better lifestyle, and yet these people were doing it without having to take accountability for anything! I was so angry and contemplated sacking off the inner work to just use people and treat them like shit to get my needs met many times. It seemed to be working for the others, so why shouldn't it for me? Then I remembered all those times in the past when I'd stopped doing the inner work and fallen back into the same patterns, and I didn't want that life anymore. I didn't want to be that person anymore, so I had to make the change, even if it meant remaining alone. When I remember why I made the decision to heal and I enjoy the benefits that healing has given me, I feel a deep sense of peace and acceptance of myself and my life. I don't feel the need to compare myself to anyone else. I don't feel in competition with anyone else. There is no need to because I have learnt that those people who haven't taken accountability for their actions and continue to blame others for their problems, will go on attracting negative experiences. They can post as many photos as possible online of this wonderful life they claim to live, but now that I know how the body and brain work, I don't believe that their happy lives are genuine and sustainable for a second.

Once I became comfortable seeing such photos on social media, I stopped being affected by them, and once I was no longer triggered, the photos stopped appearing. Life gives us something we don't like, as it shows us something we need to heal. It's a lesson we need to learn, and we will continue to find this negative thing on our paths unless we learn from it. It took me five or six months to reach a level of inner peace I'd never experienced before, and it just keeps growing slowly but surely. I have a level of self-awareness now where I can feel when something isn't right for me and act upon it, rather than suppress it like I previously did. I have no issue cutting ties with old friends or calling it off with guys who have recently tried to date me, as I understand myself now, and I understand behavioural patterns. I refused to date two very sexy guys, who both made me laugh and both had lots of great qualities, all because they weren't emotionally intelligent. I spent many years dealing with guys who weren't very nice-looking who didn't make me laugh, and had no money or career prospects, and I found it hard to end it with them because of my low self-esteem. Now, I find it easy calling it off with a guy who has all the qualities I'm seeking; if they don't have any form of emotional intelligence or self-awareness, then they need to go. It's important for me to have that, and I require that more than anything else.

Since I was five years old, I had been avoiding my pain and distracting myself from it with drugs, alcohol, and toxic relationships, but I've made the decision to face my pain head-on. It hurts, and it's scary having to feel everything I've been trying to avoid all these years. I have allowed myself to feel the pain and all the associated feelings that come with it since the end of 2022. It's been horrible re-living it, but I must feel it to heal it. I needed to be present with those feelings, acknowledge them without judgement or analysis, and only recognise them as stored energy that no longer had relevance and needed to be released.

My experiences as a five-year-old made me feel insecure, unsafe, betrayed and disgusting, and I remained feeling that way for 30 years. Therefore, I had stopped growing emotionally for 30 years. I did not transcend these emotions, so I was never free to move into the future, and when similar experiences showed up in my life (intimacy with men) those same emotions were triggered, and the same scenarios were played out in each relationship.

The more aware I am, the more present I am, and the easier it is to identify when things feel off or where I need to heal; I can take action to facilitate that. This is why I have found it easy now, to cut certain people out of my life, because I feel when someone is feeding off my energy and exhausting me. I now feel really good being on my own, and I feel so peaceful and secure. There's real power in being comfortable doing things on your own. I regularly take myself out for meals on my own or for coffee. I even went to a boxing match in London by myself. Nobody wanted to come along, so I thought, 'Fuck it—I'll go anyway!' I planned a nice weekend away in London (just as I would have done if other people were coming), booked my boxing and travel tickets, and an Air BnB. At the train station in Bristol, I got to talking with a girl who was heading to London, too, to meet a guy she'd met online. We talked all the journey to Paddington, and we had such a laugh together. We swapped numbers and agreed we would meet in London if either of us felt unsafe that weekend. When we went our separate ways, I went out for lunch before checking into my Air BnB, then had drinks whilst getting ready to go to the 02 arena. Once there, I sat at the Pepsi Max deck, where I had a waiter serve me drinks all night. I was in my element, with a double whiskey and coke in my hand, a waiter to my side and great boxing to watch all night. I loved it! I could see people and security guards staring at me as I sat by myself. I also noticed people staring at me when I walked down the corridors to the toilets each time, but I didnt care, I felt secure on my own, I was having the best time! I was so content with my whiskey and the boxing that I didn't need somebody to keep me company. I was entertaining myself!

By the time Anthony Joshua and Robert Helanius came out, the stadium was full, and some drunk lads began talking to me, which was fine, but I didn't need anyone to talk to. They invited me out after the fight, but I said no. I was happy with my own company. I took the tube back by myself at 12.30 a.m. and arrived at my Air BnB at 1.30 a.m.

The next morning, I took myself out for breakfast and did a bit of sightseeing before a nice train ride back to Bristol. I was so content and grateful that I had gone ahead with the trip despite nobody wanting to join me. Had I relied on other people to be my source of fulfilment, I never would have gone, and I would have missed out on such an incredible weekend. I also had the bonus of gaining myself a great new friendship with the girl I'd met on the train.

After, learning to seize the day by myself, I had another experience in Cheltenham. Again, nobody wanted to go, so I went by myself. I took some cans of mixed rum and coke to drink on the train, then explored Cheltenham for the afternoon. I wanted to watch England play Six Nations Rugby that evening, so I booked myself into accommodation above a pub. I ordered dinner there and watched the rugby. I ended up going to a house party with some of the locals until 5.30 a.m., and we had a great night.

Again, I'd had another fantastic time, and it was because I'd allowed myself to live and experience life whether others joined me or not. There is so much power and freedom in doing that. Life is too short to wait around for other people.

Determined that I wouldn't slip back into my old patterns, I began seeking new teachers, and I was introduced to Aaron Doughty, a spiritual teacher who began making videos on YouTube, helping people to expand their consciousness through meditations and visualisations. His range of YouTube videos were brilliant and made so much sense. I joined his online coaching sessions with spiritual coaches Mat Shaffer and Victor Oddo. These men are brilliant, and it was them who influenced me to write this book. They repeatedly said that whatever project you're thinking of starting, just start. I thought I needed to be healed and in the right relationship before I could write this book—how could I offer advice about relationships if I wasn't in the right one myself? How could I offer advice about healing yourself when I wasn't fully healed? Aaron, Mat and Victor made me realise that it didn't matter. All that mattered was that I was vulnerable and authentic. This is a gift that can be shared with others who are taking journeys similar to mine. If I can provide awareness or insight for any person and it helps and encourages them to heal from trauma, then this book has been worth it. Writing this has also been helpful to me because I have had to re-live and feel all of these feelings again with each experience. With each event I've discussed, I have learnt something about myself and identified behavioural patterns, allowing myself to heal with tools like EFT, TM, reiki, kundalini yoga and reading *The Power of Now*, (Eckhart Tolle) *A Course in Miracles* (Marianne Williamson) and *Breaking The Habit Of Being Yourself* (Dr Joe Dispenza).

This is all in conjunction with taking up new hobbies—I started kickboxing, and I love it! It has done wonders for my mental and physical health, and it's moving me in different social circles and opening up new, previously unexplored avenues. It was also through my kickboxing class that I met a neuro-linguistic programming (NLP) coach, which was an incredible bonus gift, as NLP is influential in manifesting. It was a new tool I've since brought on board to help me live the most enriching, rewarding life I could possibly have.

Writing this book has given me the strength to contact a sexual abuse support group and speak out about my experiences, although I haven't reported it to the police because it was over 30 years ago, and there's no DNA evidence to back me up. With the help of the support group, I may decide to report it when it feels right. I've accepted that there will likely be no legal justice for me, but I won't let that prevent me from healing from it. Healing is not linear—there will always be something that comes up, and I understand that now. If anybody is going through a similar experience, just know that there are plenty of us out there dealing with it in our own time. It's scary to confront this and much easier to ignore the pain under the influence of alcohol, drugs, or anything else that distracts you.

I encourage anyone with whom this resonates to use the tools I've discussed to instigate your own healing, enabling you to reach a point where you feel safe enough to speak out.

Safe to be seen and heard.

Acknowledgments

I'd like to thank every person in this book for the respective roles they played in my life, encouraging me to grow and evolve from the experiences we shared together. In particular, I'd like to thank Roxanne for encouraging me to write when we were in Australia, and Luna for introducing me to The Secret, which piqued my interest in creating a better life.

I'd like to thank my incredible team, Daniella Blechner, book journey mentor and publisher, my editor, Elise Abram, my typesetter, Amit Dey, and my designer, Emily's World of Designs. Thank you all for your patience.

About the Author

Michaela's journey is one of resilience and transformation. After facing childhood sexual abuse, leaving school with limited qualifications, and navigating anxiety, depression, abusive relationships, and financial struggles, she made the pivotal decision to take control of her life. Michaela travelled and worked across the globe, yet the emotional scars from her trauma remained. In 2022, after enduring another toxic relationship, she confronted her past head-on, focusing on healing her childhood wounds and rebuilding her sense of self. Through a year of deep personal work, she embraced her authentic self and transformed her life.

Today, Michaela enjoys a thriving career, financial stability, improved health, and fulfilling relationships. She works as an Investigator and runs her own business as an Expert Witness Environmental Health Officer. In addition, she manages an AirBnB and sells skincare products, all while continuing to inspire others through her story of courage and personal growth.

Conscious Dreams
PUBLISHING

Transforming diverse writers
into successful published authors

www.consciousdreamspublishing.com

authors@consciousdreamspublishing.com

Let's connect

www.ingramcontent.com/pod-product-compliance
Lightning Source LLC
Chambersburg PA
CBHW041138110526
44590CB00027B/4056